HEAVENLY HUMOR

for the

Mother's Soul

BARBOUR
PUBLISHING

Member of the
Evangelical Christian
Publishers Association

Printed in the United States of America.

CONTENTS

Section 1

Motherhood Isn't for Wimps: Encouragement

The Ponytail Express

JANET ROCKEY

"But the very hairs of your head are all numbered."
MATTHEW 10:30 NASB

Emily Kathryn, come here right now!" Mother shouted.

My four-year-old sister, Kathy, ran into Mother's bedroom. She stopped short when she saw me perched on the vanity stool, tears pouring down my cheeks.

"Look at what you've done." Mother raked her fingers through the spikes of what had once been my long blond hair. "Why did you cut off your sister's ponytail?"

Kathy looked up with the wide-eyed innocence only a child can produce. She pulled her hand from behind her back. The blond ponytail, still held intact by the rubber band, dangled from her tiny fingers, confirming her guilt.

"Because I got a spanking and Jannie didn't." Her matter-of-fact tone revealed her childish logic.

"Well, young lady," Mother said, "you're about to get another one!" She glared down at her older daughter and turned back to me, Kathy's three-year-old victim.

"What are we going to do with this?"

I recall my easily tangled hair had once been the bane of my mother's existence. I was so tender headed that I cried if she hit a snag. One day she pulled my hair back and wrapped a rubber band around it. She was so proud of her discovery of protecting my hair from tangle attacks that one would've thought she invented the ponytail.

She learned early in my childhood that brushing my hair put me to sleep. That is, of course, if she was first able to untangle the knots the West Texas wind tied in each strand.

"It's nap time, sweetie," she'd say in a soft voice.

"No!" I'd wail. Yes, I was sleepy and needed a nap, but there were games to play, cartoons to watch, and an older sister to pester.

"Okay, Jannie." She only pretended to give up. "Let's watch the cartoons while I brush your hair."

I sat on her lap while she combed through the snarls first with gentle strokes. Then soft bristles pulled through my hair, massaging my scalp. Soon Bugs Bunny and Elmer Fudd faded into a blur, and I unwittingly gave in to sleep.

I barely remember sitting on my mother's vanity chair—a crying three-year-old with spikes poking straight out from the back of my head. Mother resolved my hairy challenge by giving me a cute pink hat to wear until my hair grew back.

It's comforting to know that the Lord counts each strand on our heads—even the spiky ones.

Batteries Not Included

RACHEL QUILLIN

And God Almighty bless thee, and make thee fruitful,
and multiply thee, that thou mayest be a multitude of people.
GENESIS 28:3 KJV

My children recently received a bubble-blowing machine as a gift. Emblazoned across the package was the all-too-familiar phrase, "Batteries Not Included." No worries. The gift-giver had been thoughtful enough to include them. What the package failed to mention, however, is that there was also no screwdriver included. Turns out that the makers of such toys assume such a common tool is likely to be available in a home where young children reside. The problem was that we weren't at home.

So the search began. Several well-intentioned teens began rummaging through the house for something—anything—that would open this bubble-blowing wonder. What they came up with was an object that was apparently not meant to be used as a screwdriver. So now the bubble blower is stashed into a closet, screws stripped, and unable to be removed until some creative person figures out a way to get them out.

We also discovered that batteries are not the only thing absent from children's toys. Did you know that lightbulbs are also sometimes excluded? Really, they are! For my daughter's birthday, she received a candy jewelry maker, and we set out to make a sweet treat for her younger sister who wasn't feeling well. I hope the thought counted, because the actual necklace was not meant to be. You see, there was "No lightbulb included." Of course, it wasn't a typical 60-watt lightbulb that everyone should have in the home. No, this bulb would take a concentrated effort to purchase and install. Thus the candy maker claimed its place beside the bubble blower in the closet.

As I've pondered all of these tricks that manufacturers use to get us to part with our hard-earned dollars, I am struck by the direct contrast this is to God. James 1:17 (KJV) tells us, "Every good gift and every perfect gift is from above." And guess what! "My God shall supply all your need according to his riches in glory by Christ Jesus" (Philippians 4:19 KJV).

As I write this, I am thinking about our precious seventh baby, whom we recently discovered will join us soon. Already I receive many comments from strangers—some positive, some full of disbelief, and, quite frankly, some very rude. (I wonder what they would have thought of Gideon's *seventy* sons.) Most often, though, they just say, "How do you do it?" My answer is simply, "The way any Christian parent should—whether they have one child or a dozen." I realize that these children are precious gifts from God, and unlike toymakers who exclude important parts of the product, God will provide all I need to care for and raise these little ones for Him.

Other People's Kids

RACHEL QUILLIN

And all Judah stood before the LORD,
with their little ones, their wives, and their children.
2 CHRONICLES 20:13 KJV

Let's face it. It can be difficult for young children to sit through a church service. It is a learning process that, when handled properly, can lead to well-mannered children who love to attend church. That process does take time, though, and there are some people who simply don't understand that. There was a time I would have been among them.

Now I'm not really sure why I believed my own kids would sit perfectly still and sweetly pay attention to the pastor. It had never been my strength as a child, in spite of the fact that my pastor was also my dad. Still, I had this vision of my own little angels who, if they did happen to get out of line, could quickly be brought back under control by a snap of the fingers or a stern look. It didn't take me long to discover that those disciplinary measures are really not the type that will get their attention long enough to create a noticeable change in behavior. Therefore I try not to be terribly judgmental about other people's kids.

Actually I'm more apt to find the situation quite comical. I also now understand why many parents provide drawing tablets and pens for their children. So when my friends' children filed into a pew equipped with crayons and coloring books I thought, *What a great idea!* Crayons tend to be somewhat quieter than the scratch of pencils or the click of pens. Not only that, a page in a coloring book takes a bit longer to complete than a quick sketch on a spiral-bound notebook, which when completed is noisily turned to the next page. It didn't occur to me that children prefer their coloring pages to be spread flat. If the page of choice does happen to be left in the book while the young artist is at work, it will surely be removed upon completion.

I'm not sure which was the case in one particular instance. All I know is that at the exact moment that the song service ended and right before the message was to begin— at that brief interlude of time when silence generously fills the auditorium—a slow, resounding *R-I-I-I-P* echoed across the room. Immediately the young girl received a look of horror from her father (who, by the way, had to stand before the congregation and deliver the message that evening). Meanwhile, the girl's mother, her face a shade of mortified red, made her way from the piano to her seat.

Now perhaps there were those who scowled and wondered why those parents who were so active in church couldn't get their kids under control. For the most part people reacted with grins. Of course there were those who had trouble controlling outright laughter because they were just so glad it was someone else's kid—this time.

What we need to realize is that God wants families to be in church together, and families include children. All kids have to be trained how to behave in church, and the only place to teach them this behavior is in church—in spite of the glares received from those with "perfect" children.

The Sun Will Come Out Tomorrow

PATRICIA GRAU

*"But seek first his kingdom and his righteousness,
and all these things will be given to you as well.
Therefore do not worry about tomorrow, for tomorrow will
worry about itself. Each day has enough trouble of its own."*
MATTHEW 6:33–34 NIV

*D*ramatic is not a word I would use to describe myself. I like being quietly effective in the background of life. Change is something I like to plan for, and work toward, step-by-step.

However, as I gazed in the mirror the morning of my thirty-fifth birthday, I realized nature's changes were marching forward without my consent. Pesky gray strands were sprouting at odd spots, warning of more to come. I decided maybe it was time to try coloring my hair. I called and added color to my upcoming cut and style appointment. Since I was only going to cover the gray, I didn't mention it to anyone. I would just wait and see if it was even noticeable.

After cautioning my stylist against any dramatic

changes, she suggested I try auburn, a shade lighter than my natural dark brown. Auburn sounded nice. And, I had read that once the gray starts, our skin tone changes with it. The most natural look, the article said, would come from selecting a color lighter than my youthful shade had been.

With reassurances that I would love the subtle change and the healthy shine that coloring would add, I relaxed and let my stylist take over. When I looked at the result in the mirror, I saw red, not just a slight auburn shade change. I asked my stylist if she thought my hair turned out a bit too red. She waved away my concerns and again assured me I would get many compliments on the subtle change.

On the way home, glancing in the rearview mirror, I noticed my hair seemed even more reddish in natural light. I was almost in tears by the time I arrived home. The woman in the mirror didn't look like the real me. What would people say when they saw my hair?

As I stepped out of my minivan, my ten-year-old, Joseph, came running up. He stopped abruptly with a surprised look. Before I knew what was happening, he climbed on top of our picnic table and began to sing the theme song from *Annie*. Joseph belted out,

> "*The sun'll come out*
> *Tomorrow*
> *Bet your bottom dollar*
> *That tomorrow*
> *There'll be sun!*

Just thinkin' about
Tomorrow
Clears away the cobwebs,
And the sorrow
'Til there's none!"

He confirmed that my subtle auburn glinted red in the sunshine—enough that he was reminded of Little Orphan Annie. However, that song reminded me of the passage in Matthew where the Lord tells us not to worry about tomorrow. I shouldn't worry about what others might say or think. The color of my hair wasn't what defined me as a Christian. I knew that the Lord was only concerned about what was in my heart and not what was on my head.

After applauding my dramatic son, I said with sincerity, "Thank you, Joseph. That's just what I needed to hear!"

When Your Ship Comes In

MARCIA HORNOK

*"Watch out! Don't do your good deeds publicly,
to be admired by others, for you will lose
the reward from your Father in heaven."*
MATTHEW 6:1 NLT

One hot August day my daughters helped me pick the garden and can fifteen pints of sweet pickles and six pints of dilled beans. We also cut up eight quarts of cucumbers to soak in lime while my oldest son juiced a bushel of tomatoes that I made into juice and barbecue sauce.

During this strenuous day, I kept reminding myself that the virtuous woman "brings her food from afar." When I go to great lengths in working for what my family needs, I am following Lady Virtue's example. I admit, I gave myself this pep talk to stave off *is-it-worth-it?* thoughts.

At dinner that night, I asked the children, "What do you think Proverbs 31:14 means when it says that the virtuous woman is like merchants' ships, bringing her food from afar?" I wanted them to know that hard work honors scriptural principles, but I admit I had another motive—I craved admiration from them.

Nathan, my teen, answered, "Maybe it means her family looks forward to her meals."

His insight cut me short. I had mistakenly focused on the ship and the trip—my long voyage to exhaustion and back. He probably captured the primary emphasis of the verse by seeing himself on the shore, waiting with anticipation and appetite.

When we *Proverbs 31 mothers* work to provide for our family, we envision what they will need and enjoy. Thus we create meals worth waiting for, whether they be homegrown and made from scratch, gourmet cooked with expensive ingredients, or store bought and microwaved with love. Will they think to pat us on the back? Not as much as we deserve or desire. However, if we produce something inferior or late or skip a day, we'll get plenty of response. Our children will stand on the dock with megaphones to voice their disappointment.

But Jesus said that if we labor for admiration from others, we will get only that. Seeking earthly rewards sabotages eternal ones! Instead, we can please God by humbly serving our family, even though the work seems hard and endless. When our ship docks at Home Port after our excursion on earth, we want to hear Him say, "Well done, good and faithful servant." That will make all our efforts worthwhile.

Bon voyage and *bon appétit!*

Fantasyland

JANICE HANNA

As the Philistine moved closer to attack him,
David ran quickly toward the battle line to meet him.
Reaching into his bag and taking out a stone,
he slung it and struck the Philistine on the forehead.
The stone sank into his forehead,
and he fell facedown on the ground.
1 SAMUEL 17:48–49 NIV

My daughters have always had overactive imaginations. They loved to play make-believe when they were children and could entertain themselves for hours with made-up stories. One of my favorites was a play they created when my oldest was in junior high. They called it *Fantasyland*. In this whimsical tale, they were princesses who lived in a castle. Their lives were idealistic and fun. Nothing bad ever happened. Well, nothing *really* bad anyway.

They loved this story so much that they decided to videotape it. And though all of my daughters are now grown and married and have kids of their own, I keep a copy on hand, for posterity's sake. As I watch the video of my daughters and their friend, Karen, dancing around in their frilly princess-like costumes, singing the little *Fantasyland* song they wrote to go along with the play, I'm struck by how much their "make-believe" tale resonates with me. How many times have I wished I could live in a place where problems didn't exist? Where I could hide in a make-believe castle and wait for a knight on a white horse to save me? Oh, for such a place! A haven! A retreat! I would race across the drawbridge, over the crocodile-infested moat, and into the safety of the interior where nothing could harm me! Yes, there have surely been times I've longed to escape to a place where I could be safe from harm.

How are you in this area, Mom? Do you wish you could run from your problems? Pretend they didn't exist? Maybe you're facing financial woes. . .calls from bill collectors. Or perhaps you're dealing with the illness or death of a parent or friend. Maybe you're struggling with your children, one in particular. His grades aren't what you'd hoped. He's not getting along with his friends or siblings. Perhaps your spouse doesn't understand you. He thinks you're blowing things out of proportion. Maybe you wish you could climb into bed and pull the covers over your head and "imagine" your problems away.

There is no *Fantasyland*, at least not in this life. It's only a make-believe place. However, we do have a very real King who sits enthroned upon our hearts, and He longs for us to turn to Him for the help we need. Instead of running from your problems (i.e., hiding in the dungeon), run to your Father. He will give you the courage you need to face your problems head-on. That's what He wants, you know—for you to face life's challenges and rise above them. We are more than conquerors through Jesus. So, face those enemies! Lift your sword! Leave the castle prepared for battle. . .and know that the King of all kings is on your side.

SECTION 2

WHAT TO EXPECT AFTER YOU'RE EXPECTING: JOY

Dead Man Waking

RENAE BRUMBAUGH

But because of his great love for us, God,
who is rich in mercy, made us alive with Christ
even when we were dead in transgressions—
it is by grace you have been saved.
EPHESIANS 2:4–5 NIV

Isn't it funny how kids can sleep like rocks? When my son is awake, he stays on fast-forward. But once he falls asleep, he's truly in "off" mode.

My husband and I have so much fun with him when he's asleep. We lift his arms and legs and let them drop. We tickle his face. We sing songs, talk about him, and pull all sorts of pranks.

Yes, I know. That's not very nice. But it's fun anyway. And he's none the wiser, because he sleeps through the whole thing. He's even been known to sleepwalk, and we gently direct him back to his bed. It's amazing how, even in his sleep, he knows how to find the bathroom or kitchen. He's simply operating on autopilot. The next day, he never remembers a thing.

But every once in a while, when we're tickling him, he

wakes up laughing. Then we whoop and holler and make a big deal over his resurrection. "He's alive! He's alive!" It really seems like he's risen from the dead.

The Bible says that without Christ, we're like dead people. Oh, our bodies may be alive. We eat and talk and breathe. But inside, we're dead. Our spirits are sound asleep.

Sure, we may do all the right things. We may go to work every day, pay our bills, do our chores, and meet our responsibilities. Like my son, we're sleepwalking through life. We survive each day, only to get up another day and do it all again. We're living on autopilot.

But we don't need to live like that! God has made a way for us to wake up and really live. Sometimes we may feel like we have to be good enough to earn God's abundant life, but that's not true. God makes this gift available to us while we're dead in our sins. He knows a dead person—spiritually or otherwise—can't do anything to help himself out of his dead state. Only God can bring life to a dead spirit. He's waiting to lead each of us into the full, abundant lives we can experience in Christ.

God wants us to do more than survive. He wants us to thrive. He wants us to wake up and start living the abundant, rich life He has in store for all those who follow Him. Without Christ, our spirits lie dormant. With Him, our spirits soar!

Each one of us can experience wonderful, full lives. All we must do is believe God is who He says He is and believe His promises are true. Once we take that step of faith, our spirits will wake up. And that, my friends, is when real life begins.

New Spark

RENAE BRUMBAUGH

"I will give you a new heart and put a new spirit in you;
I will remove from you your heart of stone
and give you a heart of flesh."
EZEKIEL 36:26 NIV

A few years ago, my husband and I found the perfect Christmas gift for our children. It was the stuff dreams are made of, the gift nearly every kid and every adult has longed for at one time or another.

A go-cart.

It was yellow and black, with huge headlights. It reminded me of a bumblebee. It was a kid-sized two-seater, which caused some problems when Mark and I tried to test-drive it (for safety purposes, of course). There was no way we were both going to fit, so our kids watched and laughed as we, one at a time, maneuvered our way into the tiny contraption.

Mark went first. Chin resting on knees, he took off through the field of dead grass, bouncing this way and that, whooping and hollering as he went. He finally pulled back around, and it was my turn.

Now, I know what you're thinking. Our poor kids had to stand there, waiting in line, while Mom and Dad played with their new toy.

I don't see the problem.

Anyway, I squeezed my way into the miniature seat and took off. Soon I could feel the wind on my face, my hair flapping behind me. I remember wondering why I'd never considered a career with NASCAR.

I took a little longer than I needed test-driving the vehicle. (After all, I wanted to make sure it was safe for my children.)

Ahem.

Finally, Mark and I declared the thing safe, and we handed it over to our children. Never before had we heard such squeals of joy, such delight! They drove fast, they drove slowly, they practiced turning, they took turns driving and timing each other. . .man. That was one great toy.

Notice, I said *was*.

For hours, it purred like a kitten. But then it died. *Ka-put*. The motor wouldn't even turn over.

We checked the gas, the spark plugs. . . Nothing we did helped. It was dead as a doorknob. So back in the truck it went, back to the dealer.

As it turned out, there was a problem with the spark. Not the plug but something deeper. They had to take apart the entire motor to fix it.

I can relate to that little go-cart. Some days, all my get-up-and-go has got-up-and-gone. I have no spark. So I try to fix the problem myself, to no avail.

One of these days, I'll learn to go to the Mechanic at the first sign of trouble. God is the expert, and He knows how to identify the problem. He's the One who can take apart my soul and fix it. With regular tune-ups, I'll be zooming through life, whooping and hollering with joy.

Parent Heaven

TINA KRAUSE

Children are a heritage from the LORD,
offspring a reward from him.
PSALM 127:3 NIV

I thought I had died and gone to parent heaven. Hubby and I were invited to our future daughter-in-law's apartment to discuss wedding plans with her parents.

Before dinner, our son Jim offered the blessing. Then Jim and Robin whisked back and forth to the kitchen, serving the four of us hand and foot.

"Mom, can I get you more coffee?" Robin asked.

"Sure, honey," I said, hardly making a break in the conversation. Meanwhile, my son cleared the table, balancing bowls, plates, and utensils in both hands.

Unaccustomed to sitting idle after dinner, I piled dirty plates atop one another and joined the twosome in the kitchen. "Just set them down, Mom. We'll clean this up," Jim insisted as he loaded the dishwasher. "Yeah, Mom," Robin echoed, "go and sit down."

Go and sit down? We'll clean up? Was this the same son

who used to plop down at the kitchen counter, mutter, "What's for dinner?" and wait in a mummified state for me to fix his plate? What miraculous transformation occurred to change all of that?

Happily, I returned to the dining room and decided to take advantage of this rare occasion. Suddenly another surprise—Jim appeared with glass cleaner and a paper towel to clean the tabletop. "Hey, how about you guys go and sit in the living room, and we'll serve dessert," he announced with the command of a maître d'.

I beamed with a mixture of glee and pride. "This really is parent heaven," I whispered to Robin's mom as we made our way into the adjoining room.

Years of serving meals, slaving over a hot stove, cleaning up his messes, chauffeuring him to and from athletic practices, praying for him, playing with him, and loving him eventually paid off. There were times when I questioned if Jim would ever grow up. Servitude was never his strong point, but our older son turned a corner and became a responsible, sensitive, and caring man.

As I've watched my two sons grow, I've discovered that maturity isn't measured in years; maturity is measured in character. Our children are the fruits of countless prayerful nights, instruction-filled days, and our sacrificial ways. So to watch them grow and ripen into maturity is one of the greatest joys of motherhood.

"Is there anything else I can get you, Mom? More soda? Or how about another piece of pie?"

"No thanks, Jim. I'm full." Actually, my cup runneth over. Parent heaven, indeed.

Earning My Crown

MARCIA HORNOK

Gray hair is a glorious crown;
it is found in the way of righteousness.
PROVERBS 16:31 HCSB

My gray hair and wrinkled skin will finally be avenged when my kids have kids. I look forward to the day when they have children who spread dirt piles and rock collections on the front porch, moments before important guests arrive.

I can't wait until their kids cut their own bangs on the eve of school picture day and forget their band instrument on the day of the big blizzard. And hopefully their favorite song will be "Found a Peanut," which will activate every time they buckle into the family car.

Someday, no doubt, their children will reimburse them by spilling red punch on the new carpet and overflowing the toilet when they have a sitter. (She won't know how to use a plunger.)

Perhaps one day my grown daughter will find a skateboard on her child's bed—under the covers—and melted popsicles on dresser tops, and a quart of water on a closet shelf. To discard the water, she will pour it on her rubber plant. Later, her child will ask what happened to his science project about brine shrimp. Later still, the plant will die.

Will she ever find the combination to the bicycle chain locked around the stairway banister? Or learn who knocked over the aquarium or scratched the new dining room table?

If things equalize over time, my son's children will make soccer goals into the fireplace, swan dive on the master bed, and play "flashlight tag" in the dark. (I never have learned how this game is played—I only know it sends the cat hiding for three days.)

Perhaps my son will stay up until two in the morning packing the car for a family vacation. One hundred miles into the trip, he will discover that one child forgot to bring shoes. In the backseat his kids will reenact all the adventure movies they have seen (after they've exhausted "Found a Peanut"). And a crayon will melt on the driver's seat.

Yes, someday my children will get exasperated when dirty clothes avalanche from the bedrooms and the fridge door hangs open all night. But maybe instead of telling their kids, "Wait until you have children of your own," they will embrace the perspective that "Children are a heritage from the LORD. The fruit of the womb is a reward. . . . Happy is the man who has his quiver full of them" (Psalm 127:3, 5 NKJV). With this mind-set, children are not a dreaded burden that turns one's hair gray. They are God's little people. He assigns them to us so we can invest our time and priorities in what lasts for eternity.

But I still look forward to my silver-crowned years, when

my children's children will clamber for my lap. They will pat my face and ask, "Why do you have so many wrinkles, Grandma?"

I will tell them: "Those aren't wrinkles—they're laugh lines."

Wearing Crowns and Changing Diapers

VALORIE QUESENBERRY

The older women. . .admonish the young women to love
their husbands, to love their children, to be discreet,
chaste, homemakers, good, obedient to their own husbands,
that the word of God may not be blasphemed.
TITUS 2:3–5 NKJV

My oldest child is a classic firstborn—a responsible, serious, quick learner who is a perfectionist. She talked early and, though in baby language, she was quite decided in the things she was saying. Even as a child, she formed definite opinions about how things should be done. She was quite emphatic about her plans when she grew up, too. "I want to be a queen and a mommy."

Now, I'm not sure how these two things came to be connected in her mind. As a firstborn, maybe the idea of reigning over the household appealed to her. Most big sisters enjoy telling others what to do. (Being one myself, I have firsthand knowledge of this.) The mommy part of it was not surprising since she had distinct maternal qualities even then. Determined to somehow bring together the two worlds, she decided she would be a "queen mommy." It makes sense when you're three years old.

Actually, she was right on track. The Creator intended that women have a royal position in the home; it comes from following God's plan for the family.

The creative order laid out in scripture shows that man and woman were each designed for a special role—different, but noble and beautiful. Unfortunately for us, Satan used sin to attack the way the genders relate to each other. Ever since then, society has struggled with gender identity and the differentiation of roles.

The apostle Paul instructed young Pastor Titus to make sure the older women were telling the younger women the real scoop. They weren't to be social butterflies or glamour girls or sex kittens; they were to glorify God by living the life He had given them with a surrendered heart and happy attitude. Kind of flies in the face of *Desperate Housewives*, doesn't it?

Being God and the Designer of the home and human relationships, He knows how the system works best. Those who would tell us that being married and bearing babies limits our potential and fosters female oppression are sadly unaware of the truth. The abuse of women, in both the past and the present, is a result of the selfish misuse of the masculine role, not from following traditional feminine roles. Women's deserting their place does not fix the problem; it only creates a worse one.

I know it's difficult to feel "royal" when you're changing a yucky diaper or mopping up spilled juice. Not many women feel queenly with spit-up on their shirts and baby wipes in their pockets. But then, feeling isn't reality.

My little girl knew that being a wife and mother was the highest form of calling for a woman. Why? Because it's God's good plan. And isn't there an old saying that goes "The hand that rocks the cradle rules the world"? Yeah, those "oppressed" women of the past knew a thing or two after all.

So girlfriend, throw your shoulders back and walk with pride. If you're a mom, don't ever forget—you rule!

One for All

S. A. FULLER

Command them to do good, to be rich in good deeds,
and to be generous and willing to share.
In this way they will lay up treasure for themselves
as a firm foundation for the coming age,
so that they may take hold of the life that is truly life.
1 TIMOTHY 6:18–19 NIV

One of my brothers randomly beat his drums. The other one sprawled on the floor, speeding two competing Hot Wheels around a short, curvy racetrack. My new best friend, Gilda, and I sat apart from them, watching their every move. Gilda, my forty-two-inch, life-size doll, had movable arms and legs and pear-green eyes with extra-long eyelashes that she'd open or close, depending on whether she was standing upright or slightly tilted. And she kept all my secrets.

Only we knew that even though neither my brother nor I had ever played drums, I was the better drummer. We also knew that if I could spend a minute with the miniature race car's remote, I could trash my brother's theory that the red one was the fastest. It was impossible for me to get near the drums or the race kit without the two of them yelling at me, practically in unison, "Don't touch that!"

I expected their selfishness. It was Mom taking their side that really hurt. "Don't bother your brothers' *this*. Leave your brothers' *that* alone," she'd reprimand me continuously in their defense. I was convinced she liked my brothers more than me.

One day I asked her which one of us was her favorite. She chuckled absentmindedly and declared, "I love each of you the same."

Impossible, I reasoned and continued to have my suspicions. Especially on those occasions when she'd advance me a lollipop or a Little Debbie snack cake from the kitchen goody shelf, then give my brothers one as well. Even if they were outside and had no idea I'd just scored a treat, she'd go find them and make them an offer. Of course they never refused.

"If you don't have enough for all, then don't give to any," she'd tell me after noticing my displeasure.

"You need to start thinking of yourselves as the Three Musketeers," she explained. We'd recently watched the movie about the medieval band of inseparable sword fighters who defended their king and country.

"Can a girl be a musketeer?" I asked.

"Of course," she assured me. "Leave Gilda here with me," she instructed, "and go outside and tell your brothers I said so."

My brothers were playing marbles. I approached them cautiously. "Mom said girls can be musketeers," I blurted. My older brother dropped his marbles. "They can?" he questioned in disbelief before it registered that Mom was the source of my revelation. The two of them looked at each other and then at me. I turned to run.

"You can stay," my older brother conceded. "We were going to play musketeers later. Now we have all three."

That evening we swashbuckled our way to the beginning of lifelong friendship.

PARENTING WITHOUT REGRET: WISDOM

The Bell

TINA KRAUSE

Ye ask, and receive not, because ye ask amiss,
that ye may consume it upon your lusts.
JAMES 4:3 KJV

Ah, the perils of flu season. Toddlers wipe runny noses with their shirtsleeves, schoolchildren cough, sniffle, and sneeze, and kids bunk in for twenty-four hours of. . . Well, you get the picture.

Years ago when my then-small boys got sick, I'd make a bed for them on the couch. Snuggled beneath layers of blankets, they had everything they needed: a glass of fruit juice, a box of tissues, the thermometer, the television remote, and the bell.

The bell was my biggest mistake. Initially, I thought it would help the infirmed and me. Its availability to my sick son meant I could safely perform household chores in the remotest areas of our home and still hear him if he needed me. Yep, that's what I thought, and that's what he did. . . with much frequency.

Here's how it unfolded. I'd serve chicken soup and

saltines, fill the juice glass, take the temperature, dispense the medicine, fluff the pillow, and ask, "Is there anything else you need?"

Eyes transfixed on the television, my sick child would slurp down the soup and shake his head no. Confident all was well, I'd get to work for about five minutes until. . . *ring-a-ling-a-ling, ring-a-ling-a-ling!*

"What's wrong?" I'd ask, having dropped everything to run couch-side.

"Can I have some Jell-O?" he'd say, handing me the empty soup bowl.

After dishing up the dessert, I'd tuck the blanket under his chin and ask the anything-else question again.

Great, back to work. Then. . .*the bell.*

"What is it?" I'd yell through the house, becoming increasingly impatient.

In the distance I'd hear a whiny, nasal voice.

"What did you say?" I'd ask, walking closer.

"I s-a-a-a-id, I can't find the remote," he'd whimper with a look of abandonment. Without fail, the strain of having to raise his voice weakened his body as he struggled to position himself with feeble movements. Amazingly, one tiny porcelain bell turned an otherwise dutiful child into an ornery, self-centered brat.

In much the same way, God gives us the privilege of prayer—the proverbial spiritual bell to communicate with Him anytime, anywhere, about anything. But instead of approaching Him with our adoration and praise, we often bombard Him with a long list of requests. Although God desires to answer our petitions, our selfish motives often get in the way, and we miss the whole point of prayer.

After repeatedly misusing the bell, my son finally got the message when I refused to answer. Eventually, I confiscated the *ring-a-ling* altogether.

In the flu season of our lives, God administers the instrument of prayer. He listens, willing to heal our spiritual infirmities, but He may not always answer the way we'd like. Nevertheless, the bell stays because, unlike a pushed-to-the limit mom, the Lord is long-suffering.

Achoo! I mean, amen. Thank God for that!

A Hodgepodge of Growing Things

ANITA HIGMAN

"Martha, Martha," the Lord answered,
"you are worried and upset about many things,
but few things are needed—or indeed only one.
Mary has chosen what is better, and
it will not be taken away from her."
LUKE 10:41–42 NIV

When my daughter, Hillary, was around ten years old, she asked if she could have a small spot in the backyard for making a garden. She wanted to experience the pleasure of planting seeds and watching things grow. I was happy for her to enjoy the outdoors, learn to care for living things, and satisfy her curiosity surrounding the miracle of God's creation. All good stuff.

Until Mom got involved. *Mercy.*

I wish I could talk about *Mom* as if she were someone else—a sorry little person who lived down the street, and who wore chartreuse garden clothes and smelled of manure—but I have to admit, it was *me.* Instead of pointing to a place in the backyard where my daughter could begin her adventure,

I "helped" her with the project, orchestrating a garden that could be photographed for one of those home-gardening magazines.

We'd purchased the best soil, lots of plants, and even a garden bell to ring. Talk about over-the-top, especially since my daughter didn't want beautiful landscaping; she just wanted a spot of earth to call her own.

Of course, you can imagine what happened over time. Hillary stopped weeding her garden. She stopped enjoying its beauty. And then she stopped going to visit it altogether. Why? With all the work I put into my daughter's garden to make it Martha Stewart perfect, it really turned into *my* garden and not *her* garden. So, instead of celebrating the fun of a hodgepodge of growing things, it turned out to be just another bed of flowers in our backyard that had nothing to do with fun.

My sad tale reminds me of the famous Mary and Martha story in the Bible. Martha was the harried one who whirled in the kitchen, wanting to impress Jesus with her culinary skills, while Mary just wanted to be near Him and listen to whatever He had to say. To be honest, I'm a Martha type, so I always think, "Surely Martha had a good heart, too, wanting Jesus to be well fed and to feel welcome." But I'm also a Mary wannabe, so I know what appears to be good on the outside may not be the wisest choice at the moment.

So, back to my daughter's garden. I apologized to Hillary for railroading her dream, and she forgave me. But sometimes I think back on that incident and remind myself that I'd focused so intently on the beauty of my daughter's garden that I wasn't paying attention to the beauty of our relationship.

Sometimes God is more interested in my relationship with Him than the good intentions written in my day planner. Hard lesson for us Martha types. But in that close relationship with the Lord comes the really good stuff—being in our Savior's presence, hearing that mighty, gentle, and awesome voice that can challenge hearts and change lives, and that sweet communion that gives us a momentary glimpse into eternity and brings heaven a little closer to home.

The Thornbuds

JANET ROCKEY

Train up a child in the way he should go,
even when he is old he will not depart from it.
PROVERBS 22:6 NASB

Our mother had three children close in age. Jimmy, the eldest, was Chief Tormentor. Making his sisters cry was his sole aim in life. Kathy was in the middle. I was fifteen months younger than Kathy.

Daddy called us his *three-ring circus*. Mama, with a wink to Daddy, called us *thorns in her side*.

One morning, when I was four years old, Mama sliced half a banana over my cereal. She turned to slice the rest over my sister's bowl.

"No!" Kathy wailed, spreading her hands over her bowl.

Mama pulled back in surprise. "You don't want banana on your cereal?"

Kathy folded her arms across her chest. "Not *that* banana."

"What's wrong with this banana?"

Kathy pouted. "You cut it over *her* cereal first."

Mama sighed. "Honey, Jesus wants you to love your sister." She held the banana over the bowl again.

Kathy's bottom lip jutted out. "I don't care. I don't want *that* banana."

"Okay, young lady, eat your cereal plain." Mama sliced the rest of the banana over her own bowl.

I shoveled Cheerios into my mouth, delighted to see Kathy getting reprimanded.

Then I annoyed Kathy by staring at her.

"Mama! She's looking at me again!" Kathy yelled.

I turned away in feigned innocence. "What?"

By the time Daddy came home from work, he saw only our slightly askew halos and couldn't fathom what Mama endured all day with us three thorns in her side.

When we weren't fighting, we were conjuring up trouble. Kathy and I once used the home office answering machine to record a plea. "Rescue us from the witch who locked us in our room!" Daddy's customers were puzzled. Mama was not amused.

Jimmy's lizard got loose and found a good hiding place in Mama's shoe. Mama screamed like a banshee and danced a jig.

The glass on the ant farm broke. That was a fun day.

Soon enough, her thorns became teenagers.

"Kathy's trying to steal Greg from me," I cried to Mama. "He liked me until he met *her*. . . ." I pointed to my sister. "The *pretty* one."

"A boy with wandering eyes? You should doubt *his*

character, not your sister's," Mama said. "And you're both pretty," she added.

Kathy turned up her nose. "Greg's a conceited child."

I didn't know she'd aimed her sights on "Sugar Bear," an older boy in her English class.

Mama listened to us pierce each other with barbed words. "I pray one day you'll love each other," she said.

Then Mama injured her back.

We three *thorns* formed a coalition. Taking over the chores Mama could no longer do, Kathy and I cooked and cleaned. Jimmy mowed the lawn. Daddy took care of everything else.

The morning after Mama came home from one of her surgeries, Kathy and I made breakfast.

"Want to share this banana with me?" Kathy asked, holding the uncut fruit over my cereal bowl.

"Yes, thanks," I answered.

Mama smiled at the evidence of her answered prayer. Yes, God can sprout buds from thorns. She taught us the way of the Lord, and when we matured, we didn't depart from it.

Grass Hogs and Raccenhoons

RACHEL QUILLIN

And out of the ground the LORD God formed every beast of
the field, and every fowl of the air; and brought them unto
Adam to see what he would call them: and whatsoever
Adam called every living creature, that was the name thereof.
GENESIS 2:19 KJV

One of my favorite parts of having young children is encouraging them to appreciate the beauty and wonder of God's creation. It is so much fun to watch their expressions as we visit zoos, wildlife areas, or nature museums. Discoveries made by young, impressionable children are refreshing in comparison to the jaded attitudes of many adults. Every butterfly, pinecone, or smooth stone is a special treasure in their eyes.

I guess it's no wonder, then, that I find it so much fun to teach my kids the names of animals and the sounds they make. What little one doesn't enjoy a good round of "Old MacDonald Had a Farm"? Just thinking about my two-year-old's rendition of "cock-a-doodle-do" and "hee-haw," not to mention his imitation of a lizard or rabbit, is enough to make me smile. Have you ever noticed the voice inflection and facial expressions of children as they tell you what each animal says or does? It's almost as if, for a brief second, they are putting themselves in that animal's place.

You know, when God created the animals, everything was perfect. I sometimes wonder what Adam must have felt like surrounded by all those beautiful, peaceful animals. What was he thinking as he selected just the right name for each of God's creatures? I don't know what language he spoke or how long it took him to complete the task, but I can imagine it was probably one of the most delightful jobs in which he ever engaged.

I suppose, then, that because we don't know exactly what Adam called each animal, it is acceptable that our children sometimes generate their own names for them. The only problem is that we run the risk of not really knowing what they are talking about. For instance, when my son was about three years old, he was helping Daddy farm. He came home all excited, exclaiming, "Mommy, we saw a grass hog!" I looked blankly at my husband, who mirrored my expression. We knew our son loved pigs, but that didn't seem to be what he was referring to.

All at once it dawned on us. Apparently a groundhog had waddled across the road in front of them. I realize that most people aren't crazy about groundhogs, but small children just don't have that same cynicism. He was thrilled.

Another of my kids' favorites when they were smaller was the "raccenhoon." We have an abundance of them, and the kids saw many pictures as well. Their coined name for the raccoon was a bit easier to decipher. I knew I needed to teach them to speak properly for their own good, but it was a bit difficult to correct them on that one. I was almost sad when they learned to say it properly.

The truth is, we could all learn something from the little ones. We could all stand to feel a bit more awe as we consider God's creation.

I Want to Be a Zookeeper

RACHEL QUILLIN

*Whether therefore ye eat, or drink,
or whatsoever ye do, do all to the glory of God.*
1 CORINTHIANS 10:31 KJV

All children have ideas about what they want to be when they grow up. It seems as though firefighters, police officers, nurses, and teachers often topped the list as I was growing up. Perhaps that is because they were highly visible and rather exciting career options in the eyes of a child. Those are still valid and often-sought-after dreams, but it seems that kids today have a wider perspective of the possibilities available. Maybe it's due in part to the fact that those who *did* become teachers, in an attempt to maintain job security, have introduced "career exploration" and "community helpers" into their curriculum. Pretty tricky, but the kids do love it, and it does open their young, impressionable eyes to a whole new world of opportunity.

Here's a case in point. My own family is filled with firefighters and health-care professionals, but not one of my children has any inclination toward these fields. My eldest has declared that he wants to be a paleontologist. (There are just so many of those around!) Of course, he has enjoyed many dinosaur digging kits, is the proud possessor of several large herds of these behemoths, and has quite an extensive library on the subject, so it is only natural that his dreams would lie in that direction.

My eldest daughter's dreams are vastly different from her brother's. She lives, breathes, and dreams art in one form or another. It probably goes back to her debut moment when she was a toddler. I went to get her up from her nap and much to my horror discovered that she had been painting the walls and floors with the contents of her diaper. We made sure that option was eliminated, and her choices of medium are now much more hygienic with her current favorites being anything involving fabric, needle, and thread.

Then there is number three, whose blood runs John Deere green. His first word may well have been "tractor." He spends hours perfecting his one-sixty-fourth-scale farm and deems time farming with Daddy of far greater importance than math or reading. In all honesty I'm not sure he is aware of career opportunities other than farming.

Finally, we come to our dear, sweet four-year-old who, in the same breath, declares, "I want to be a princess and a zookeeper." I'm really not sure how well those two combine unless she plans to keep a collection of kissable frogs. I have assured her that if she puts her mind to it, she can be almost anything she wants to be. Somehow, though, I'm pretty sure princess would not be included in the list of possibilities. A zookeeper, on the other hand, might truly be a career worth pursuing.

I know that our kids could change their minds hundreds of times before they actually decide on a career path, but we need to always encourage them to do their best—for God's glory—and we need to set the example for them ourselves.

Jerky

RACHEL QUILLIN

He that hath knowledge spareth his words:
and a man of understanding is of an excellent spirit.
PROVERBS 17:27 KJV

It has been a very long time since I went anywhere without having to get numerous people ready. As a result, I tend to forget what that is like. It seems to me that a grown adult who has only to get himself ready to be somewhere should really have no excuse for tardiness. Apparently my expectations are too great.

I had set up my baby's portrait session for the earliest appointment. I do this intentionally so that we will not have long waits resulting in cranky babies at the studio. The appointment was at ten o'clock, which certainly seemed reasonable to me. The idea was for my mom and brother to meet me in the studio parking lot. They would pick up the older children for an overnight visit with Grandma and Grandpa. That would be much more fun for them and would make it easier for me to concentrate fully on the baby during her portrait session.

I knew it would take a little while to get car seats, bags, and all manner of kid gear transferred from one vehicle to another. I really didn't want to forfeit my early appointment by showing up late, so I made sure to arrive a little early. We settled in for what should have been a few-minute wait.

We waited. . .and waited. . .and waited some more. I began to wonder if maybe I shouldn't have told them that the appointment was at nine thirty. Of course, I knew this wouldn't have mattered. I knew exactly what was going on. My brother had gotten off work, and instead of just coming to get my kids, he felt it necessary to feed his horses first.

I began to mutter. It got closer and closer to appointment time, and I began to seriously contemplate just taking all the kids in with me. I'd certainly done it before; there was no reason not to do it again. I knew my time was limited, so I began to unbuckle seat belts. If my AWOL brother ever showed up, he could just come in and find me. Then *he* could wait until the baby was done getting pictures taken. Once that was done, we would get the other kids' things—if I was still willing to let them go.

However, as the kids began to unload, I saw my brother pulling in. By this time, I was really fuming. It didn't occur to me in those moments of weakness that my young children picked up everything I said and were fully capable of repeating it. So as I was tossing things out of my van and grumbling about what an inconsiderate human being my brother was, my little sponges were absorbing every bit of the information. My son couldn't wait to share with Uncle Dave that Mommy said he was a "jerky." In fact, it was the first thing he blurted out upon my brother's arrival.

I felt like such a fool. It might be true that my brother hadn't behaved in the most responsible way, but then again, neither had I. I was frustrated, even angry, but the example I set for my kids that day was hardly mature, let alone Christlike.

Inside Out

JEAN FISCHER

Create in me a pure heart, O God,
and renew a steadfast spirit within me.
PSALM 51:10 NIV

If Pat's kids want to ride on the backs of elephants, eat chocolate-covered beetles, or hang out with storm chasers, it's fine with her. I've asked Pat more than a few times, "Don't you worry about them?"

"Not really," she says. "God is in control. I'm just His zookeeper."

With five kids at home between the ages of three and sixteen, Pat's house qualifies as a zoo.

Her middle son, Frederick James (not *Fred* or *Freddy*), wants to be a veterinary surgeon someday. So when he asked permission to use the family's dog, Chauncey, for his science fair project, Pat agreed.

"I'm going to paint Chauncey to show what's inside of him—his skeleton and internal organs and stuff," Frederick James said.

"Fine," his mother replied. "Use washable markers, and

take your time. If Chauncey gets antsy, give him a break."

Chauncey is a small dog, a smooth-coated fox terrier. His sleek, white fur made the perfect canvas for Frederick James's artwork. It's a good thing that Chauncey is laid back and easygoing, because Frederick James's project required that the dog sit very still.

The ten-year-old went straight to work. Using a gray, thick-tipped marker, Frederick James drew in the dog's skeleton, beginning on the snout with the lower maxillary and ending on the hind feet with the metatarsus. Then he carefully outlined all the major internal organs and colored in each one using a different colored pen. The end result was worthy of a canine anatomy textbook.

At the science fair, reactions were mixed. Adults admired Frederick James's accuracy and artistic ability, but the kids laughed at the brightly painted dog. By the end of the evening, Chauncey hung his head with shame.

"Poor Chauncey," Pat whispered to her son.

"Aw, Mom," Frederick James answered. "He'll get over it."

Frederick James took third prize, and Chauncey earned a bath. Pat gladly agreed to do it as a reward for Frederick James's hard work.

At home, she put Chauncey in the bathtub. She wet down his wiry coat and started to scrub. . .and scrub. . .and scrub! Frederick James had used permanent markers.

The poor dog walked around for weeks inside out and utterly humiliated. If anyone pointed or laughed at his graffiti-like coat, Chauncey crawled under the bed and whimpered. All he wanted to do was hide.

What if everyone could see what's inside of you—not your skeleton and organs but what's in your heart? Would you be embarrassed for your family and friends to know your secrets and see your sins laid bare? Would you try to hide from God, like Adam and Eve did when they discovered their nakedness in the Garden of Eden?

We may be able to hide from others what's inside of us, but we can never hide it from God, our King.

Just Ducky

Jean Fischer

A gossip goes around telling secrets,
but those who are trustworthy can keep a confidence.
Proverbs 11:13 NLT

My neighbor Fran liked sleuthing the neighborhood checking that everything was okay. If anything unusual went on, Fran knew right away, and she didn't keep secrets. Most of the neighbors avoided Fran, and I did, too. I didn't want the neighborhood to know all my business.

It was around dusk when Fran knocked on my front door. "You won't believe what I just saw," she said dramatically.

"What?"

"A duck flew into your yard. A great big duck!"

She stretched her arms to show a wingspan like an eagle's.

"Should we go see?" she asked.

"Um, the fence gate is closed, and it's getting late. . . ," I rambled. I didn't want Fran rummaging around my backyard.

When I left for work the next morning, I saw the duck waddle under a shrub. I went to look, and it burst out and flew away in a shower of feathers. Under the shrub I saw a nest with six pale blue-green eggs.

It's okay, Mama Ducky, I said to myself. *This will be our little secret.*

I kept that secret, too. If Fran knew that Mama Ducky was camped out in my backyard, the whole neighborhood would know it. I didn't want a parade of people coming to see the duck and scaring her away from her nest.

Finally, early one morning, I heard a faint peeping sound coming from under the shrub. The ducklings had arrived, six adorable soft babies. I left for work feeling like a proud auntie. Mama Ducky and her children were just fine, and I'd done a great job protecting them.

Or so I thought.

When I arrived home later and drove into my driveway, I almost ran over Fran. She stood by my fence gate holding a garbage-can lid like a shield, pounding on it with her fist making an awful racket. On the other side of the gate, Mama Ducky squawked angrily and flapped her wings. The ducklings stood behind her, frightened, in a tight little bunch. I tried to hide how annoyed I was with Fran.

"What are you doing?" I asked gently.

"Help me!" Fran wailed. "She's trying to leave with the babies."

"That's what ducks do," I said. "Let them go."

She gave me a disbelieving look. "Let them *go*?"

"Yes, Fran," I said firmly. "She'll take them to the pond

down the street. Let them go."

Fran stood aside and allowed Mama Ducky and her babies to pass. She insisted, though, on following them, and of course she told people along the way. Soon there was a parade of children chasing Mama Ducky and her ducklings to the pond.

The apostle Paul warns about going house to house, gossiping and being a busybody. We need to heed Paul's warning. The Bible says that no human can tame the tongue (James 3:8), but certainly we must try.

In Case of Emergency, Break In

Donna K. Maltese

There is a time for everything. . .
a time to be silent and a time to speak.
ECCLESIASTES 3:1, 7 NIV

My mother had a few strict rules, one of which was, "Never interrupt adults when they're talking." This was an arduous restriction for three talkative little girls. Nevertheless, Mom trained us well and was soon blessed with *kidsus noninterruptus*.

One summer while we were at our beach house in Avalon, New Jersey, the Foxes, our friends and neighbors, came to visit us for a week. One afternoon, Benny Fox, who was a year older than me, and I decided to ride our bikes on the boardwalk.

We were having a great time riding the boards, the sea wind in our hair and the sun on our faces. At the end of our jaunt, I headed for the ramp nearest our block. Before I knew it, I was flying down the slope at top speed. There was a brief bounce as the ramp ended and my tires hit the sidewalk. I braked then looked behind me to check on

Benny. As he hit the ramp, one of his pedals flew off. Next thing I knew, he and his bike began to wobble. As Benny struggled to maintain his balance, he gained the sidewalk but then lost control of his bike and—*wham!*—drove straight into a telephone pole.

Benny lay on the sidewalk, groaning and bleeding from his nose and mouth, his mangled bike at his feet.

I stood over him in shocked silence for a few seconds, then finally gathered my wits. "Benny! I'll go get your mom!" I jumped back on my bike, crossed the street, and drove two houses down to our shore home. I ditched my bike and ran up the stairs to the dining room where I found Mom and Mrs. Fox in conversation. Knowing I was not allowed to interrupt, I waited till there was a lull in the conversation. As I waited, I heard the siren of an ambulance in the distance. I began to shift my weight back and forth as the siren grew louder and louder.

Mom noted my obvious impatience, yet continued in her conversation. Finally, the women stopped talking.

Mom turned to me, not a little irritated. "Well, Donna, what are you so anxious to tell us?"

As the siren winded down, I blurted out, "Benny ran into a telephone pole. He's lying on the sidewalk, bleeding from his nose and mouth."

Mom looked incredulous. "You're kidding!"

"No! No! He lost his balance coming down the ramp from the boardwalk, hit the pole, and. . ."

By this time, Mrs. Fox was running to the door, my mom following right behind, yelling, "Why did you wait so long to tell us?"

"You told me never to interrupt!"

Mom stopped in her tracks and turned to face me. "Okay. Listen carefully. New rule. In case of emergency, break in."

Mom's rules are great. Where would we be without them? Yet rules must be tempered with wisdom. In this life, there is a time to speak and a time to remain silent. Hopefully, as seasoned Christians, we know when to swallow our words and when to use them. It's all in the timing.

"Right Behind You, Blab"

DONNA K. MALTESE

Careless words stab like a sword,
but wise words bring healing.
PROVERBS 12:18 NCV

When we were growing up in the 1960s, my sisters and I never missed Hanna-Barbera's *Quick Draw McGraw Show*. One of the cartoons featured on the program was "Snooper and Blabber." Super Snooper was a cat detective; Blabber ("Blab") Mouse was his partner. An oft-stated line of Super Snooper's was, "Right behind ya, Blab," a bit of dialogue that my sisters and I often repeated to each other in conversation.

Of course by the time my son, Zach, was born—in the 1990s—the show was history. But I've found that when you have children of your own, you regress a little bit into your own childhood and remember trivial things from that period of time. So I began saying to Zach the things I'd spoken during my own early days of life.

As a very young boy, Zach was a bit on the husky side physically, so we encouraged lots of exercises, one of which was walking to the bus stop. On elementary school days, I'd wake him up in the morning, help him get dressed, feed him his bowl of oatmeal, and help him get his backpack ready. At some time during the morning, I'd look at the clock and tell him it was time to head for the bus stop located on the corner of our block. He'd don his coat and backpack and then, before heading out the door, turn to me and say, "Come on, Mom. Let's go."

My standard response would be the quote from Super Snooper and Blabber Mouse: "Right behind you, Blab."

Morning after morning like this went by. Zach would say, "Come on, Mom. Let's go," and I would respond with, "Right behind you, Blab."

Finally one day we went through the routine: "Come on, Mom. Let's go."

"Right behind you, Blab."

But this particular morning, Zach stopped and stood there, very still. As he looked at me, his tiny lip began to tremble and tears formed in his eyes.

Immediately I got down on my knees and looked him straight in the face. "Honey! What's wrong?"

"Mom," he said in a timid little voice, "will you please stop calling me 'Blob'?"

My heart leaped into my throat. I felt terrible. "Oh, honey, I'm not calling you *Blob*. It's *Blab*. It's from a cartoon show I used to watch when I was a kid. *Super Snooper and Blabber Mouse*."

He looked a bit confused. It was almost like he didn't believe me.

So I gave him a big hug of reassurance, but later I wondered how devastated he must have been each morning, thinking I was calling him a blob. Yikes! From that day on, I never again used that line.

It's amazing how much what we say affects people—especially those words spoken between a mother and her child. There we must be extra careful, for what we mothers say has a deeper impact on our children than on anyone else. And when they are young, they may not understand the exact meaning of the words we speak.

So herein is the lesson: Speak clearly and choose your words carefully.

Know-It-Alls

DONNA K. MALTESE

Trust GOD from the bottom of your heart;
don't try to figure out everything on your own.
Listen for GOD's voice in everything you do, everywhere you go;
he's the one who will keep you on track.
Don't assume that you know it all.
PROVERBS 3:5 MSG

In the beginning of their lives, children think their parents are perfect and know everything. Then somewhere along the line, things change. Parents know nothing, and the kids know it all!

Such was the case with our oldest. In her teens, Jennifer saw us as not only imperfect, but terribly dense and out of touch with the "real" world. We knew absolutely nothing, and she knew it all.

A few months after Jen graduated from high school, we set her up with her own checking account. My husband, Pete, and I sat her down at the kitchen table, ready to explain exactly how to use it.

We began with, "So do you know how to write checks?"

"Yes"—she rolled her eyes—"of course I do."

Biting our tongues, we proceeded. "Well, this part of the checkbook with all the rows and columns is called a register. When you write a check—"

Jen heaved a sigh.

With extreme patience, Pete said, "I'm sorry. Are we boring you?"

"Well, yes."

I took over. "So you know what to do with the register and how to balance your checkbook?"

"Uh, yeah. They showed us in high school."

"Okay. So, we're done here then, I guess," replied my other half.

She nodded, swiped up the checkbook, and walked out of the room.

Pete and I looked at each other. I said, "Well, that went well."

A few months later, Jen came home from her freshman year at college. While she'd been away, she'd bounced a few checks that'd we'd then had to cover her for. So Pete finally pried the checkbook loose from her hands and studied the register. Again, we were in the kitchen.

Pete said, "Jen, you never recorded your checks. How did you ever balance your checkbook?"

"I didn't have to."

I said, "Well how did you know if you had enough money in your account?"

She rolled her eyes again. "Because I *still had plenty of checks*."

It's amazing the things moms think their children automatically know, only to find out later that they *don't* have a clue how the "real" world works. Instead, our kids use some convoluted logic to figure things out.

Although we can't be exactly sure what our children actually do understand, life experience reveals the gaps. As moms, all we can do is pray that God will help it all come out right and make sure we're there to catch our children when they fall.

Our life experience *can* make us wiser than our kids. Yet there's no way that we children of God can comprehend everything our heavenly Father knows. All we can do is trust in His leading and understand that some day, when we're with Him, He'll explain everything. For He truly is the ultimate Know-It-All.

Surprises

S. A. Fuller

*Then we will no longer be infants, tossed back and forth
by the waves, and blown here and there by every wind
of teaching and by the cunning and craftiness of people
in their deceitful scheming. Instead, speaking the truth in love,
we will grow to become in every respect the mature body
of him who is the head, that is, Christ.*

EPHESIANS 4:14–15 NIV

Victoria had the grown-ups fooled. They were putty in her hands because of her occasional church solo. In between the elaborate hoaxes she engineered to embarrass me and get a laugh from our seventh-grade classmates, she'd manage a spiritual standard at Sunday service and have the entire congregation raising their paper fans to the ceiling and shouting "Hallelujah!"

I wasn't impressed. I refused to be moved by her Sabbath-day transformation from *hell's spawn* into *voice-of-an-angel crooner*. I muffled my giggles as she stretched notes like spandex and repeated lyrics as if it were mandatory until raised fans gave way to heat and exhaustion.

Mom usually initiated the ovations following Victoria's padded renditions. Her praises didn't end with the song though. She went on about Victoria's good manners and pleasant nature like she walked on water. Mom saw right through my tiniest white lie but was completely blinded by brown-nosing Victoria's contrived preference for her barely edible cooking and disingenuous compliments of her overly floral Sunday hats.

Every summer Victoria and I worked through our rivalry on a local farm. Earl usually drove us home on the back of his pickup. On the way home one day she boasted that she could run home as fast as Earl was driving us there.

"No you couldn't," I challenged.

"Bet I could," she countered.

"You could, too," she coaxed.

"I'm not jumping off the back of a moving truck," I argued.

"On three, we jump," she said, starting a slow count and sliding closer to the edge of the tailgate to give herself the advantage. . . .

At "three," I jumped and started running.

I looked up to see where the truck was and saw Victoria still sitting on the tailgate, laughing and pointing at my gullibility. I ran as fast as I could, but suddenly it seemed as if Earl was clocking autobahn speed and the truck was miles in front of me. It was impossible for me to catch up to it. After a while, I saw brake lights. Earl looked back at me standing in the middle of the road gasping for air in bewilderment.

Victoria had scored her biggest *gotcha*. It was weeks before my leap of faith stopped being sidesplitting and gossip worthy. That's when Mom mentioned it. "Maybe next time you'll take everything Victoria says with a grain of salt like I do," she told me with a wink and a smile.

I thought that if she knew about the truck chase, she would reprimand me for risking my life. I never expected her to make light of it or prove that she knew the real Victoria.

My mom never stopped surprising me.

SECTION 4

LIGHT AT THE END OF THE LAUNDRY CHUTE: BLESSINGS

Going Coconuts

Renae Brumbaugh

All hard work brings a profit,
but mere talk leads only to poverty.
PROVERBS 14:23 NIV

The kids and I recently cracked open a real, honest-to-goodness coconut. Wal-Mart had them for $1.50 each, and the kids looked at me with puppy eyes, so I figured, why not? It'll be fun.

Famous last words.

We got the coconut home, and the kids took turns shaking it, listening to the liquid inside. I didn't have a clue how to crack the thing open. I was imagining coconut milk spilling all over my floor, when I noticed a little tag on the coconut.

There were instructions.

I had never bought fruit that needed instructions before.

The tag said, "Drain milk through soft eye." I didn't know coconuts had eyes. I located three eyes; none of them felt soft. I got a screwdriver, and voilà! Two holes punched right open.

But the milk doesn't just pour out. You have to shake it out. And while shaking, you must try not to spill it all over everything.

I had a coconut milk bath. I wonder if there are antiaging properties in there. . . .

Next, the instructions said, "Pound open at groove." Sure enough, there was a groove. Do they grow that way?

I pounded it on the counter.

Nothing.

I pounded it with the screwdriver.

Nothing.

I pounded it with a hammer.

Still nothing.

Finally, my daughter suggested I pound it with the claw end of the hammer. Sure enough, *crrrrrraaaaaack!*

Getting the milk out was easy, and pounding it open was a piece of cake compared to the next phase.

The meat of the coconut (Did you know it is called "meat"?) is sealed inside, apparently with superglue. I looked at the tag. No more instructions.

I spent the better part of an hour getting that meat loose from the shell, piece by tiny piece. The kids were long gone, playing in the backyard while their dear mother slaved away on the coconut they had so desperately wanted.

By the time I finished, I had furry coconut hairs all over my clothes, my hands were sore, and I was starting to wonder what lunatic had taken over my body when I agreed to buy the thing.

Then I tasted it. Delicious! It tasted nothing like the

furry white stuff that sits on top of a cake. I decided all the work was worth it.

You know, the best things in life rarely come without sweat and elbow grease. Whether it's a great marriage, a successful career, or a long-lasting friendship, the good stuff never comes easily. Progress seems slow, coming bit by tiny bit.

But if we hang in there, we'll eventually reap the benefits of our labor. The success earned from endurance and hard work is sweeter than the easy store-bought variety. In spite of the rough spots, the mess, and the difficulties, the end result is always worth the effort.

Getting Shots

RENAE BRUMBAUGH

Consider it pure joy, my brothers and sisters,
whenever you face trials of many kinds,
because you know that the testing of
your faith produces perseverance.
JAMES 1:2–3 NIV

I smiled at my son. "Would you like to visit the fire station today?"

"No thanks."

"Really?" I asked. "You'll get to see fire trucks."

"Naaaah."

"It's a special day. There'll be a bouncy house."

"I'd rather not."

I was perplexed. "Why not?"

"Because I heard you and Jay's mom talking. It's a big trick. They're giving shots there today."

That's one smart kid. *Brilliant.*

In spite of protests from both my children, we visited the fire station. We ate hot dogs and snow cones. We saw a clown. And, yes. We got our immunizations.

Well, I say *we*. But I mean *they*.

In spite of the distractions, the shots still hurt. But I was impressed with both my children. They didn't even cry (much).

Later, Mark and I decided our kids deserved a treat. I mean, in addition to the bouncy house and snow cones. We took them to Chuck E. Cheese's. By the time we finished eating, the kids were running around playing, contributing wholeheartedly to the restaurant's decibel-breaking noise level.

Personally, I'd rather have the shots. But this wasn't about me, and the kids loved it. I think they'd probably even say the shots were worth it, just so they could go to their favorite eating establishment.

Later, Foster asked, "Mom, what's an im–im–iminemation?"

"Well," I responded, "an immunization is a teensy bit of a disease. It's like a bad guy. When your body sees the bad guy, it makes a bunch of high-powered fighters called antibodies. They run off the bad guys and make sure they never come back. So if that disease ever enters your body again, they'll be ready."

"Oh," he said. "They hurt."

"I know, buddy."

As much as it hurt to see my children in pain, I was relieved to know they're protected from nasty diseases like rubella and diphtheria. The immunizations weren't pleasant. But the results created strong, healthy children who won't be affected by any number of diseases.

Sometimes in life, we must get our shots. They come in the forms of all kinds of nasty situations. A nail on the road may cause a flat tire; a poor economy may lead to a job loss; for no known reason, we could be diagnosed with cancer or worse.

Yet, if we let God have His way, He'll make sure the bad guys work like immunizations to our spirits, calling forth strength that may have been lying dormant, a strength that comes only from God. Before we know it, we'll be handling our problems with a greater strength than we ever thought possible.

Yeah, shots hurt. But when God is in control, He'll use those things to make us stronger, wiser people. In the end, we'll end up saying that yes, the shots were worth the pain.

Toasted Turtles and Other Minor Calamities

ARDYTHE KOLB

She watches over the affairs of her household
and does not eat the bread of idleness.

PROVERBS 31:27 NIV

"Mommy! There's a. . .um. . .a hippopotamus in the backyard." That definitely got my attention, though I had my doubts.

Four-year-old Debbie grabbed my hand and called to her brother, "Kevin, come see!"

"Look!" She pointed to a possum that was pretending to sleep. *Hippopotamus* and *possum* do sound similar, I suppose.

I backed up, easing Debbie and Kevin away with me as I explained, "That's a possum. He has sharp teeth and might wake up really grumpy, so let's not get too close."

We returned to the kitchen and discovered my youngest child, Marshall, sitting on the table in a puddle of milk, cereal, and syrup left from breakfast. Any thinking mother knows never to leave an eighteen-month-old unattended, even when there's a hippo outside. Marshall giggled as I scooped him up and headed for the sink, trying to keep him from dripping along the way. I stripped off the sticky clothes, rinsed him off, and dressed him in a clean outfit. We then headed for the toy box to find something interesting to occupy him so that I could restore order to the kitchen.

A few minutes later a voice came from the bathroom. "Mommy, Marshall's playing in the potty!"

Abandoning the kitchen project, I raced down the hall. Kevin stood back, obviously enjoying the fact that Marshall was the one in trouble. Wet toilet paper was festooned from wall to wall, and the remainder of the roll bobbed in the toilet, along with Tigger, Marshall's favorite stuffed animal. He hit the flushing lever again.

"What am I going to do with you?" I said, tiptoeing through the soggy mess. We headed back to the toys. "Kevin, can you keep him happy while I clean things up?"

What kind of insanity was that—putting a three-year-old in charge of his baby brother? I almost had the bathroom back to normal when Kevin's voice rang out, "Mommy, Marshall's on the kitchen counter!"

Sure enough, he was on his knees, peering into the toaster. Our toaster is activated simply by dropping a slice of bread (or in this case, our silver-dollar-sized pet turtle named Ted) into the slot. Amazingly, Ted was still among the living when I flipped the appliance upside down to shake the poor creature free. Liberated from his tormentor, he seemed happy to return to the confines of a fishbowl.

Marshall was ready for his next adventure, but I'd had

enough for one morning. I picked up a Dr. Seuss book and called Debbie and Kevin. "Let's sit down and read a story." I leaned back and involuntarily let out a huge sigh. Debbie gave me a peculiar look and said, "You wanted to be the mom."

Whether that was a question or a statement, I wasn't sure. But it's true. Nothing is more fulfilling than the God-given calling of motherhood. Most days.

And mothers certainly don't "eat the bread of idleness."

The Big 3—0

JANET ROCKEY

Behold, children are a gift of the LORD,
the fruit of the womb is a reward.
PSALM 127:3 NASB

Let's go!" Daddy shouted.

We scrambled from the living room. Nine-year-old Jimmy dashed out first, claiming the "shotgun seat" in Daddy's Rambler.

My sister, Kathy, almost seven, ran out the door ahead of me. She wore one shoe, carrying the other in her hand.

I was five and a half and followed her with a brush stuck in my hair. In the backseat, Kathy freed the hairbrush from my tangles. Like Prince Charming, I slipped the shoe onto her bare foot.

Daddy winked at us in the rearview mirror. "Make sure you each pick out something really special for Mommy." Our mother's thirtieth birthday had arrived, and he offered to let us shop for her gifts.

We chattered as he drove past the line of stores on the square in downtown Brownfield, Texas.

"What're you gonna buy?" I asked my sister. She shrugged. "I dunno."

Daddy parked in front of Fields Department Store and herded us inside, greeting the salesman with a polite "Howdy."

An hour later, we piled into the station wagon, clutching our purchases. Next stop—our grandparents' house to wrap them. Then home for lunch, ice cream, cake, and presents.

After our meal of hot dogs, Mommy opened Grandmama's gift. "Oooh, a wedding ring quilt," she said. "Thank you, Mother."

Kathy and I pointed out remnants of outfits she had made for us. Even pieces from Jimmy's shirt framed the edges.

"My gift was staying out of her way while she made it." Granddaddy chuckled and handed Mommy a check.

Daddy gave her a large, oblong package, wrapped in shiny white paper. Mommy opened it and smiled. "Joe, it's beautiful." She pulled out a sable mink stole. "Just beautiful!" She held it close, stroking it as she leaned over to kiss him.

Granddaddy wolf-whistled. He turned to Grandmama. "No, you can't have one. You're not thirty."

All the adults laughed.

My brother handed Mommy his gift, wrapped in cowboy-print paper.

"You wrapped this yourself, didn't you?"

"Yep!" Jimmy beamed.

"An archery set," she said, opening the box. She strummed the bow's elastic string and reached inside for the stopper-topped arrows. "Thank you, Jimmy." She hugged him and kissed his cheek.

Mommy opened Kathy's gift. "Oh, how sweet. A Betsy Wetsy doll. . .with a bottle and diapers." She hugged and kissed my sister. "I haven't changed diapers in a long time."

I had rolled up my gift like a mummy in Cinderella paper.

Mommy unwrapped the stuffed toy skunk. "Pepé Le Pew. Isn't he cute?" She touched the fabric bouquet in his hand. "And Pepé brought me flowers."

I got a hug and a kiss, too.

She set her "adult" gifts aside and carried Jimmy's archery set to the backyard. We took turns shooting the target. She gave Betsy her bottle and showed Kathy how to change the doll's diaper. She pretended to speak French to Pepé Le Pew and sniffed the flowers he offered.

My mother's face glowed with happiness. "This is the best birthday I've ever had," she said when she tucked us in that night. She blotted a joyful tear and said, "I love your presents, but you children are my most precious gifts from God."

Forever Young

Janet Rockey

Bless the LORD, O my soul, and forget none of His benefits. . .
who satisfies your years with good things,
so that your youth is renewed like the eagle.
PSALM 103:2, 5 NASB

My mother was full of surprises. She sprang the first
surprise on me at a family gathering when I was a youngster.
She started off her sentence to a relative with, "When I was
a little girl. . ."

I dropped my doll in surprise. "You were a little girl?"
I asked wide-eyed.

The grown-ups chuckled.

I thought she had always been—and always would
be—a grown-up. My childish reasoning also dictated that
I had always been—and always would be—a child.

"Yes," she answered, "I was a little girl."

"A long time ago," her cousin Malcolm added.

She laughed with him and then turned back to me
with a grin. "And one day you'll be a grown-up."

A sob hid behind my quivering mouth. "Will you still

be my mommy when I grow up?"

She wrapped me in her warm hug. "Sweetie, I will always be your mommy."

In the years to follow, family members shared more of Mother's surprising stories with me.

"I remember you saying the blessing when the pastor came for dinner," Grandmother said to my mother one day. She turned to me before Mother could respond. "When she was five, she surprised us all with her prayer before a Sunday dinner. Palms together, she bowed her head and prayed, 'God the Father, God the Son, and God the Holy Ghost. The one who eats the fastest gets the most. Amen. Let's eat!' "

Grandmother's younger sister Fay added her two cents, too. "When your mama was six, I took her on a train trip. Children five years and under traveled for free. As we waited for the train to stop at our destination, the porter patted her on the head and asked, 'How old are you, little girl?' She smiled up at him and said, 'I'm five right now, but as soon as I get off this train, I'll be six again.' "

Her younger cousin Malcolm reported that in the summer of '44, she badgered him with constant requests to play his 78 rpm record, *A Guy Named Joe*, over and over again.

"She let it slip that she'd just met a guy named Joe at a soda fountain in Lubbock," he explained with a wink. "The Mighty Eighth Army Air Corps brought him from Philadelphia here for training."

In those days, an eighteen-year-old girl didn't travel

alone. Her mother and sister chaperoned her trip to visit the guy named Joe after his transfer to Savannah, Georgia. Her father admonished her, "Don't come back engaged, young lady!" She surprised him by coming back as a bride.

I grew up, but she never grew older—or so it seemed to me. She remained the same mommy who broke the earth-shattering news to me that children don't stay children and that adults were once youngsters. No matter what health obstacles life threw in her direction, her youthful glow and quirky humor persevered.

She went home to be with the Lord shortly after her fiftieth birthday. As much as I miss her, I view that as a blessing. In my mind and my heart, she will always be forever young.

Return to Sender

JANET ROCKEY

"For where your treasure is, there your heart will be also."
MATTHEW 6:21 NASB

"Mrs. Cummings is on the phone, Mama," Kathy said.

Mama picked up the receiver my older sister had placed on the breakfast bar. "Hi, Jo. I was just about to call you. . . . Yes, I noted it on my calendar. . . . I'll have everything boxed up for him. . . . Thanks for calling, Jo." She hung up the phone and turned to us children. "Let's go through our things to see what we can give to the church rummage sale."

"What kind of things do they want?" Kathy asked.

"Oh, toys, clothing, books. . .anything that you don't mind giving to a worthy cause."

Kathy and I hugged our Barbie dolls to our chests.

Mama glanced at our dolls. "Toys and clothing you've outgrown."

Jimmy, our older brother, offered the lawn mower.

Mama laughed. "No, I think we need to keep that. But I'm sure you've got a few things someone wants."

"What about the Howdy Doody dolls?" Jimmy asked.

"You killed them, remember?" Kathy said.

"Did not."

"Did, too."

"Did not."

"Did, too."

"Enough!" Mama stomped her foot, ending the perpetual debate. "Now, go find some treasures to donate."

Jimmy headed down the hall. "Did not," he whispered over his shoulder.

Kathy and I ambled to our room. My sister picked through our toy chest while I went through the closet.

An hour later we carried our cast-off goods to the living room. Mama sat cross-legged on the floor in front of the bookcase. Jimmy sat next to her, arranging items in the box to make room. She had already gone through the kitchen. The saltshaker that had no mate and a porcelain cream pitcher with a red rooster painted on it were wrapped in tissue paper to protect them from breaking.

She sighed. "I shouldn't be so attached to these books." *Moby Dick* and an ancient-looking *Longfellow* accompanied *Bleak House* and *Kipling's Best*. She handed each to Jimmy. He set them, spines up to show their titles, in the corrugated box. "Good-bye, old friends," she said.

A twinge of guilt washed over me. I gave up toys and clothes I didn't want anymore. Mama donated things she cherished. A glance at my sister and brother confirmed they shared my unease.

Ding-dong! "That'll be Jo's husband," Mama said,

looking at her watch. "And right on time, too."

"Wait, Mama," I said. "There's something else we can give."

The three of us dashed back to our rooms. Kathy and I came out with our Barbies. Jimmy followed with his baseball glove.

Mama stayed home from the rummage sale that year, but Daddy dropped by on the way home from his golf game.

"Look at what I found at the rummage sale, Gerry!" he called to Mama from the garage. He carried in the box of treasures he had bought. "These are classics!" He pulled out each book to show her. *Moby Dick, Longfellow, Bleak House,* and *Kipling's Best.* "And. . . I found a mate to our saltshaker. And this creamer. . .don't we have a sugar bowl that matches it?"

Mama shook with laughter.

I peered into the box. Two Barbie dolls and a baseball mitt completed his booty.

Mama stored her real treasures in heaven as she taught us the blessings of sacrificial giving.

Hooked

PATRICIA GRAU

"Therefore I will praise you,
LORD, among the nations;
I will sing the praises of your name."
2 SAMUEL 22:50 NIV

My son loved to sing, literally, from the day he started to talk. During a visit when he was three, my mother-in-law asked, "Have you noticed that Joel sings *on key* when he sings along with recorded songs? Most young children learn to mimic the lyrics, but few can copy the tones."

"Actually, I hadn't noticed anything more than his enjoyment of music," I said. "As you know, when his dad and I sing, it's definitely *making a joyful noise* rather than singing. Do you think Joel's been blessed with a musical talent?"

She said, "I do. And I'm sure the Lord will make use of his talent. "

The following year, Joel started preschool. While watching their Christmas musical, I realized Joel had the main speaking part. After the show, with a hug I told him how much I enjoyed his performance. Then I asked, "Joel, why didn't you tell us you had a big part in the show?"

"Mom, I just did what the teacher asked me to do. That's all."

"Well, doing what your teacher asks is a good thing." I guess it seemed like a bigger deal to me, a person more comfortable behind the stage, than it did to Joel.

When Joel was nine, he asked if he could audition for the youth theater that had visited his school. His dad and I replied, "Sure, if that's something you think you'd like to do." At the audition, Joel seemed to have fun while I, as an observer, felt anxiety race through me.

Although Joel landed a minor role in *Peter Pan,* he was on stage for most scenes and was one of four cast members who flew. After the final show, Joel told me he was *hooked* on musical theater. He laughed as he clarified, "Did you get it, Mom? You know, *Captain Hook!*"

"Yeah, I get it—you're hooked." Actually, I didn't get it. I couldn't imagine how a child of mine could come alive when he was performing on stage. Once *hooked*, it was off to dance lessons in preparation for more stage roles. And by fourteen, he had his first adult chorus role at the local opera house.

In addition to theatrical roles, he taught himself to play the guitar. And yes, he formed a band with two of his Christian buddies. Although I can't say I appreciated their loud version of music, I started to see Joel's ability to lead others when he performed.

At eighteen, Joel was singing and playing guitar for our

church praise and worship team. When I saw him witness his faith at church, through his music, I truly saw his God-given talent shine. Now, finally, many things made sense. Joel had been *hooked* by his God-given musical talent, not musical theater. Performing was the Lord's way of developing and strengthening Joel. The result was a man who loved God and could sing His praise to others.

God Gives Me More

VALORIE QUESENBERRY

"Give, and it will be given to you. A good measure,
pressed down, shaken together and running over,
will be poured into your lap.
For with the measure you use,
it will be measured to you."
LUKE 6:38 NIV

Children are naturally stingy. Let's admit it—they are little Scrooges from the womb. From the moment of delivery, they think of themselves first. And of course we don't blame them for that—it's part of infancy. Yet, as they grow, it's a mother's task to carefully and prayerfully train them in the virtue of sharing.

My children, like yours, were uninterested in bettering their characters in this way. They generally saw no need for it. The grace of selflessness was not their highest aim. I have often pondered how different parenting would be if children were born without an inclination to please self.

As a mom, I usually live in a state of hope—hoping that my children are "getting" what I've been trying to teach them. Occasionally I taste a bit of panic. "What if they don't get it?" The ongoing sibling rivalry, the bickering, and the perpetual race to get the front seat, the shower, the biggest piece of cake—selfishness wears on a mother's mental health and makes her wonder if she will ever civilize these little beings the Bible refers to as the Lord's *reward*.

Occasionally I glimpse a ray of light in the process. And I start to believe that maybe, after all, my kids will turn out to be godly, productive adults.

My second daughter was born beautifully bald. Over the next few months of her life, she acquired a cap of downy blond fuzz that made her look like a cute little peach. Her older sister had been blessed with adequate locks since birth. She sported enough hair to make adorable little ponytails and fluffy curls for Sunday.

I guess she must have developed a feeling of pity for her sparsely coiffed baby sister. And maybe she was picking up on the "sharing" thing more than I realized, but I didn't expect what was coming. Imagine my chagrin one day when I found them sitting together—the older one with scissors and jagged self-cut bangs, the younger one with tufts of brown hair lying atop her little head.

I asked the classic "mom" question. "What are you doing?"

Her reply? "She needed hair. Jesus will give me more."

What do you say to that? How do you reprimand a toddler for sharing her abundance with one who is in need!

I'm sure I tried to explain to her that Jesus would give her sister her very own hair. And maybe I wondered if her words were a noble-sounding cover-up for playing with the scissors! But she was right—Jesus did give her more, though she looked a bit strange with little sprouts of hair in the meantime.

Like my toddler, I should share my blessings with others, believing that if I distribute what I have, God will replenish my supply. He rewards those who give, not those who hoard.

And perhaps it's no coincidence that today my oldest daughter has luxuriant, healthy hair. After all, He promised abundance in accordance with the measure we use to give. She deserves a head full!

Goldfish Temptations

Valorie Quesenberry

"Which of you, if your son asks for bread, will give him a stone?
Or if he asks for a fish, will give him a snake?
If you, then, though you are evil, know how to give good gifts
to your children, how much more will your Father in heaven
give good gifts to those who ask him!"
MATTHEW 7:9–11 NIV

Has your child ever eaten goldfish? I don't mean the little orange crackers. I mean the real thing—the kind that have fins and live in a glass bowl. My daughter did once.

Once upon a time, our family owned three goldfish. They were lovingly named Cinderella, Snow White, and Sleeping Beauty. They spent their days in a glass bowl on a dresser in the bedroom of two little girls. Unfortunately for the fish, the mommy of the little girls wasn't very dutiful about cleaning out the bowl. As the water became cloudy, the oxygen content dwindled. They were obliged to jump from the bowl and take their chances on the nursery floor beyond.

Sadly, one of the little girls hadn't yet learned to walk.

So she crawled everywhere, stopping to pick up interesting bits of stuff and put them in her mouth for further exploration. The mommy, being preoccupied with dressing the big sister, didn't even notice what the baby was chewing on until she reached to take it out of her mouth.

Yuck! It was a poor goldfish—lukewarm and quite limp after time spent on the dry carpet. The mommy was horrified, but the baby wasn't concerned in the least—the soft, rubbery thing felt nice on her little gums. The little girl was exploring her world, and she didn't have the wisdom to know that you shouldn't taste everything you see.

In a spiritual sense, I may be tempted to do the same thing. As God's child, I have more growing to do. I'm still learning. I have a limited perspective. In my immaturity, I may reach out for a wonderful tidbit that looks inviting, not realizing that Satan is deceiving me.

I'm reaching for goldfish every time that I. . .

- base my worth on a magazine article rather than God's perspective.
- feed my mind with cultural opinion instead of biblical truth.
- spend my energies on getting rather than giving.
- trust my own wisdom instead of asking for His.
- swap faith for intellectual philosophy.
- allow my priorities to get confused.
- neglect my time alone with Him.

We are God's children. He feels about us like I felt

about my daughter gnawing on a stiff goldfish. "Put that down! I've got something so much better for you!" He sees what we sometimes miss—that the world's dainties are really full of decay.

Like any good parent, God provides what we need. The Bible says He doesn't give us stones or snakes; He gives us good things. He delights to shower us with blessings. But to receive them, we have to ignore what's at eye level and look up. The goldfish on the floor can't tempt us if we focus on Him.

"BECAUSE I SAID SO" AND OTHER SOUND ADVICE: OBEDIENCE

Birthday Blunders

ARDYTHE KOLB

We all make many mistakes.
For if we could control our tongues, we would be perfect
and could also control ourselves in every other way.
JAMES 3:2 NLT

Family birthdays blur in my memory. We had a Christmas baby, one born on December 21, and the other three in September and October. By the time birthdays and Christmas were over, I felt tattered.

You'd think no parent could forget a birthday, but when it coincides with Christmas Day and the child is only two, it can happen. We enjoyed a full day, but at bedtime Debbie said, "Isn't today Kevin's birthday?" I'm so thankful for children who keep tabs on me. It wasn't really as bad as it sounds. We celebrated a month early with presents and cake, but the actual day almost got away without a word.

After that, I had nightmares. I'd forget to buy Christmas or birthday gifts for one of my offspring. It was a different child in each dream, depending on—I don't know—maybe a nagging sense that one of them felt neglected that day.

But my worries never kept birthdays from being celebrations. With seven people in our household, we really didn't need anybody extra to make a party, so we decided that each child would have only two birthdays where they invited friends.

Debbie didn't think that was such a good plan. When she was seven—a nonparty year—she arranged her own without telling us. I don't know how she thought she would pull it off, but we learned about it the day before. A mother called asking, "Do you need any help for Debbie's party?"

"What party?"

"Her birthday party tomorrow."

"What party?"

"You mean you don't know she's invited her friends for a party?"

"No."

"She lied! Well, if that's the kind of child she is, I don't want Cynthia to play with her anymore!" And she hung up.

Debbie and I had a long discussion, but because of that mother's attitude, we had a party anyway. And it was fun. Without Cynthia.

Years later, we'd added another daughter. I was preparing for Kristin's third birthday, and she naturally wanted to help make her cake. The ingredients were on the countertop when she pulled her chair up beside me. Before I realized what was about to happen, she picked up an egg and smashed it against the surface. Without a pause she turned to me with a totally innocent expression and said, "Oh-oh! Look at Erik do!" She hadn't mastered the fine art of passing the buck.

(Erik was at school, and I was an eyewitness to the crime.)

But as the youngest, she learned at an early age to speak up and find a convenient scapegoat.

Who hasn't spoken without considering the consequences? Our tongues can bless, or they can get us into trouble. An unplanned party and broken egg became teaching moments but certainly didn't eliminate the temptation to utter untrue or unkind words. Ask the heavenly Father to help you guard your tongue today.

Too Much to Ask?

TINA KRAUSE

*Son though he was,
he learned obedience from what he suffered.*
HEBREWS 5:8 NIV

When our sons were growing up, my husband and I planned our vacations around the places and activities that were of most interest to them. However, I insisted that at least one day be spent touring something historical. Apparently that was too much to ask.

"Not another pioneer village," they moaned. Historical translated into hysterical as smiles faded and energy levels plummeted. "It's Lincoln's childhood home," I explained, which immediately initiated a whining session.

"Do we have to go?" they would ask.

"Do I have to watch you drive the go-carts? Do I have to play arcade games with you? Do I have to jostle my innards on roller coasters and risk my life careening down waterslides? Do I. . . ?"

"Okay, Mom," they grumbled. "We'll go."

But they made me pay. Big time. Our day of tourism

consisted of four hours of one-way family interaction. With exaggerated sighs, the boys walked as fast as garden slugs, shuffling their feet.

"Hey look," I said with exuberance, scanning the brochure. "It says here that this is the log building where Lincoln first practiced law." No one responded, not even Hubby. As we strolled through another exhibit, I turned to my husband to share a morsel of historical trivia, hoping to lighten the air. "Uh-huh," Jim replied, forcing a grin.

Soon I noticed father and sons commiserating. Jim consoled the kids, whispering things like, "I know, I know. It won't be long now. Mom's almost done, and we'll go to the pool when we get back to the hotel."

You'd think I sentenced them to forced labor. Over lunch I tucked the pamphlet beside my plate to chart our next destination.

"I'm hot," son Jeff whimpered.

"We're in air-conditioning," I said through clenched teeth.

"So how much more is left to see?" Hubby asked not so discreetly.

With that, I stuck the brochure inside my purse and announced that we would leave right after lunch. Suddenly chatter and peals of laughter filled the table. The temperature was perfect, the setting divine, and I was no longer vacationing alone.

Interestingly, children (and sometimes husbands) opt for the selfish side of life. But perhaps we mirror their actions more than we realize. The Lord blesses us even when we don't deserve it, yet we insist on having our way. When life takes a difficult turn, we grumble, lose our spiritual enthusiasm, and shuffle our feet in despair. Instead of trusting God, we pout and complain until, in reluctant surrender, we say, "Okay, Lord, I'll do it."

The Father never asked His Son, Jesus, "Is it too much for You to face ridicule, rejection, false accusations, and a brutal scourging? Is it too much for You to die for the very people who hate You?" Instead, Jesus willingly obeyed.

God expects from us what we expect from our children, namely, willingness and obedience. Is that too much to ask?

Simple Requests and Memory Loss

TINA KRAUSE

The spirit indeed is willing, but the flesh is weak.
MATTHEW 26:41 KJV

Okay, listen up, everyone. After you shower, please wipe down the tile." It wasn't an unreasonable request, just a simple, time-saving gesture so that I could engage in other activities besides scrubbing, disinfecting, and polishing.

For two whole days, my then-teenage boys adhered. After that, it became too much for their bulging muscles to handle. That's when excuses flowed like molten lava from Mount Kilauea.

"But I wasn't the last one to shower," son Jeff protested. "Besides, I'm running late. I'll do it later, Mom." I've heard that before. "Later" as in sometime-long-after-Mom-buffs-the-tile-squeaky-clean-and-it-doesn't-need-wiping-down-anymore "later."

Somehow simple requests were the hardest for my two sons to follow. Sudden memory loss occurred when I asked them to take out the garbage, feed the cat, or stack the dirty dishes in the dishwasher instead of piling them—caked with food scraps—in the kitchen sink.

"Oops, sorry I forgot" was a common phrase that was supposed to trigger immediate clemency from me. Yet these same guys had photographic memories to recall all the words to their favorite songs, individual batting averages, or what recreational activities they planned for three weeks from Saturday.

In the same way, God has a few simple requests for us, too, such as read your Bible, pray, obey God, and love one another. These are reasonable requests, yet some of us are like teenagers when it comes to following through. "I'm too busy," we say. "I'll do it later when I have more time." Or in an attempt to invoke God's immediate approval, we confess, "Oops. Sorry, Lord, I forgot."

Yet interestingly, we remember what time our favorite television program comes on, recall what hours the mall is open, or what day we have off work. We know what we should do, but we often fail to do it. Good intentions are meaningless without corresponding actions—much like my sons' failed promises.

So I wiped down the shower tile—again. Seems my request needed an incentive. This time I thought I'd try the memory-loss excuse—be apologetic yet insincere.

When my son returned home that day, he asked if anyone called as he scanned the stove top for signs of dinner.

"Sorry, I forgot," I responded with wide-eyed innocence.

"Forgot who called, or forgot dinner?"

"Both. I just didn't have time, son."

"Well, when do we eat?"

"Later, Jeff. . .much, much later."

Amazing. He quickly regained his memory.

Going to the Real Camp

PATRICIA GRAU

*May he give you the desire of your heart
and make all your plans succeed.*
PSALM 20:4 NIV

Joshua had a mildly successful T-ball season the summer between first and second grade. Based on this information, our second-grade son decided he didn't need school; he was going to grow up to be a professional baseball player. No matter how we encouraged him to take school seriously, he didn't seem to respond. I prayed that he would grow out of this phase quickly. However, each marking period, his teacher expressed her concerns about Joshua's lack of priority on learning.

We tried to explain to our seven-year-old that even professional baseball players needed a good education. But Joshua was confident that he would be successful as an athlete regardless of how he did at school. Joshua begrudgingly completed his assignments, making second grade a painful family experience.

Then in March, the Sunday school had a special

gathering day where all children were welcomed in the fellowship hall. As an assistant teacher, I sat in the back as the high school class conducted an overview of the upcoming summer church camps. Joshua sat in rapt attention in front of the cardboard campfire as the older kids shared fun experiences from attending church camp.

At the conclusion of the gathering, the youth pastor distributed pamphlets with sign-up forms. He carefully reviewed the requirements for each of the camping opportunities. He explained that once children successfully completed a grade in school, they were qualified for the grade level they would begin in the fall.

First and second graders would take a daily bus to and from a local camp for three days. For third and fourth graders, camp was a three-day experience that included two overnights, sleeping in a cabin.

As we headed to the worship service after Sunday school, Joshua handed me his camp registration pamphlet. He said, "Mom, don't lose this. I want to go to camp this summer."

Walking to the van after church, Joshua asked his dad and me, "Do you think it's too late for me to pass second grade?"

"What?" we replied in unison.

"Well, I have to graduate from second grade! I want to go to the third-grade camp where you stay two nights in a cabin. They're not fooling me; the camp for second graders where you go for the day on a bus is just day care. That's not a real camp."

"I guess it's all up to you," I said. "Joshua, you know the Lord wants you to have the desires of your heart. But He expects you to work for what you want."

The very next day, Joshua enthusiastically embraced school. He was a child with a plan to succeed.

Soon enough, Joshua loved his three-day, two-night camp for third graders!

Stolen Candy

JANICE HANNA

"But if you fail to keep your word,
then you will have sinned against the LORD,
and you may be sure that your sin will find you out."
NUMBERS 32:23 NLT

It was one of those hot summer days in South Texas where the kids spent all afternoon splashing around at the pool and moms counted the hours until school would begin again. I'd had my fill of heat-induced kid antics but—being the fun mom on the block—always found my nest filled with neighborhood children, as well as my own three daughters.

A midafternoon trip to the grocery store provided the opportunity to keep the kids busy and pick up a few necessary items. My nine-year-old daughter's best friend asked to tag along. For whatever reason, my girls decided they all needed to wear their cowgirl boots. They seemed pretty determined. Didn't make a bit of sense to me, especially since they were all wearing shorts and T-shirts. Still, kids will be kids. Right?

We shopped for nearly an hour, filling the basket with

the usual fare. I did my best to keep a watchful eye on the girls as I shopped, but they wandered a bit, giggling as they slipped from aisle to aisle.

Imagine my surprise when we arrived at the register to pay for the groceries and I looked down to find a candy bar peeking out of my oldest daughter's boot. My gaze quickly shifted to my middle daughter's boot, where I found more candy. Then my youngest. Still more candy. Same with my daughter's best friend. Four little boot-wearin', candy-stealin' thieves stood before me, sure they'd gotten away with their crime.

I looked at my oldest and hollered, "Are you stealing from this store?" I pointed to her boot, and her eyes filled with tears. I continued to rant, going from child to child, boot to boot. All of the candy was laid on the conveyor belt, and I spoke to the clerk using my sternest voice to further intimidate the kids. "My children are stealing from your store. I want you to hold them accountable. Do whatever you need to do."

She looked at me, eyes wide, and I could read the sympathy there. After all, the kids had been caught. The candy was safely handed back over to the store. Clearly this overly compassionate woman had no plans to call the police, or even the store manager. Instead, she just shook her head, took the candy bars, and put them back on the candy rack with a shrug.

I sighed. Then with new resolve, I decided to join her in extending grace to my children, offering them forgiveness and motherly kindness. Of course there would be consequences, but the public humiliation had probably offered enough incentive to never repeat the crime.

Have you ever hidden your sin away, hoping your heavenly Father wouldn't find you out? Ever thought you could get away with it, only to have His glaring spotlight shine down on the very thing you were trying to hide? If so, welcome to the club! We all sin and fall short of the glory of God. Like our children, we all let "Daddy" down. We do things we shouldn't. Instead of 'fessing up, we run and hide.

Next time you're tempted to hide your candy in your cowboy boots (i.e., sin in secret), rethink your plan. Your sin will find you out. Why not get things out in the open where God can deal with them—and you.

Lose the Guilt;
Find the Kid: Faith

Misplaced Children

ARDYTHE KOLB

"Can a mother forget the baby at her breast
and have no compassion on the child she has borne?
Though she may forget, I will not forget you!"
ISAIAH 49:15–16 NIV

I never exactly forgot a child, but there were a few times when one was temporarily misplaced. With a tribe of small people, shopping could be overwhelming.

"Can I have some candy?"

"I need to go potty."

"When are we gonna be done?"

Every mother knows the routine.

One day I loaded our groceries into the car, herded the kids into their seats, and took the cart to the corral. I'd climbed behind the steering wheel and backed out of my parking space when Kevin asked, "Are we gonna take Erik home?"

I slammed on the brakes, did a quick head count, and realized that Erik, our youngest at that time, was still in the grocery cart. *What kind of a mother am I?* My heart pounded as I raced back to retrieve him, positive he would never forgive me. I hugged him close and looked around to see if anyone noticed. This was before security cameras, so at least I didn't worry about seeing my mug shot on the evening news.

We lost Erik another time, but that wasn't my fault. Well, not entirely. The kids were all playing outside, supposedly keeping track of him. But when they eventually came in, he didn't.

I said, "Where's Erik?"

"I don't know."

"Weren't you watching him?"

"I forgot."

"Where was he when you saw him last?"

"I dunno. Can I have a snack?"

I searched the yard, the sidewalk, and the street. "Erik, where are you?" Neighbors joined me, and we were ready to call the police when I spotted a bit of blue, the color of his outfit, under a bush a couple of houses away. There he sat, wearing a big grin, watching all the activity. (I never could punish a child who had been misplaced—even if he was being ornery. It's a time for hugs.)

There were other memorable missing-child incidents. Debbie followed a dog into his little house in a neighbor's backyard one day when I thought she was in her bedroom. Kevin crawled behind stacks of paper towels in a grocery store, watching our desperate hunt. Marshall tried to find his way back to our old house after we moved and sat down to cry when he realized he was hopelessly lost. And we were nearly home from a Bible study one night before we realized we had left Kristin behind.

Each time led to panic, extreme relief, and embarrassment. How could a mother let her child slip away? Scripture asks if a mother can forget her baby. That may seem impossible, but it happens. We can forget to hug children enough, forget to listen closely when they want to talk, or forget to take time just to play. In our busy lives, we often forget the most important things. Thank heaven for our wonderful Father, who never forgets any of His children! Praise Him today!

The Best Part of Camping

ARDYTHE KOLB

For You, Lord, are good, and ready to forgive,
and abundant in lovingkindness to all who call upon You.
PSALM 86:5 NASB

Most mornings I cajoled, bribed, and offered to do my children's homework to coerce them into eating something—anything—for breakfast. The homework idea didn't help; they wanted to pass.

But by six o'clock on the morning when we were camping, everyone was famished. Simply boiling water on one of those little green two-burner stoves was a challenge. Preparing bacon, eggs, and hash browns for seven people took a miracle, but that was the expected menu. Working in cold, damp weather while padding through wet grass in flip-flops and making multiple trips with kids to the outdoor facilities added a special flair.

To keep us on our toes, signs dotted the campground with pictures of bears: DANGER! DO NOT STORE FOOD IN TENTS. We didn't want large, furry critters breaking into our sleeping quarters, so we hauled everything out of the van for meals.

For our first camping experience, we borrowed a tent that was recycled from a Boy Scout troop. (Don't ever try that. It had no floor.) We set it up on a slight slope, and during the night our children kept rolling out. That wouldn't have been so bad except for the rain that started about midnight. Wet sleeping bags take a long time to dry.

I opted for no more camping but was voted down. And I admit, pine woods, beautiful beaches, and long hikes made up for simple inconveniences like poison ivy, mosquito bites, and the occasional snake.

The kids loved one particular spot in Wisconsin, situated beside Lake Michigan. It's always cold, so we gathered near the campfire at night, which led to the endless warning: "Stop playing in the fire! You'll burn the woods down."

Of course my husband was the one whose sneaker caught fire.

Lake Michigan's water is never warm enough to swim, but as one of the children said, "It's not bad once you get numb." That only took seconds. I wouldn't have considered going in, except that was the only place to get wet all over at a camp with no running water.

The real joy of camping came years later when our grown children decided to have their own great-outdoor adventures. They straggled home saying things like:

"The Coleman didn't work, so we ate at McDonald's."

"A rowdy party kept us awake all night."

"We forgot the tent pegs!"

"The girls wanted to go to a motel."

Our daughter summed it up: "Mom, camping was such fun when we were kids. What changed?"

When I read about the forty-year wilderness camping trip in Exodus, I try to picture what the experience was like. Would I have murmured? No doubt! I'm awed by our God. He forgave the Israelites' bad attitude over and over, and He does the same for us no matter how much we whine or complain.

Motherly Mechanisms

Tina Krause

When she speaks, her words are wise,
and she gives instructions with kindness.
Proverbs 31:26 NLT

I'm convinced that mothers possess inherent mechanisms that fathers just don't have. One of them is the ability to predict how soon school will start without ever looking at a calendar. Each year near mid-August, an invisible mechanism triggers a jolt to our nervous system that signals the beginning of the school year.

Throughout our sons' childhoods, summers were terrific until about two weeks before school was due to start. Similar to the arthritic patient who is able to predict rain, I sensed the back-to-school season in my bones.

A transformation took place as I underwent strange personality changes. I gnashed my teeth, clenched my fists, and counted to ten as my kids' behavior gnawed at me like hungry termites feasting on rotting wood. Petty annoyances became aggravated assaults on my well-being— sibling arguments turned into major warfare, and normal noise levels morphed into exaggerated explosions.

I blamed the kids, but was I the problem?

I recall one summer day when my then-fourteen-year-old son was acting like his normal teenage self. Apparently I had failed to notice his knack for slamming things until then. Jeff thumped through the house like an overactive monkey bouncing from one surface to another. Whatever he touched, he slammed—*loudly*. Lids, drawers, and cabinet doors were not merely closed, they were unhinged. So much so that each time he opened the kitchen cabinet, shock waves reverberated through me.

Clang! Boom! (I winced.) "Jeff, take it easy."

"What?" he replied, which in teen language means, *"I have no idea what you're talking about so you figure out what 'what' means."*

"You know what? Stop slamming doors," I said sternly.

"I'm just getting a glass."

"I know, Jeff. Now knock it off."

"What?" (There's that word again.)

"Jeff, I can't concentrate with all that noise!"

Tugging my hair, I reached for the calendar to confirm my suspicions. Instinctively, I knew the first day of school couldn't be far off. "Ah, yes. Two weeks before school starts and the house is again MINE, MINE, MINE!"

Later on when the kids were asleep and I had time alone, I sank into an overstuffed chair to read God's Word. *God*-cidentally I opened to the book of Proverbs and read about the virtuous woman. At first read I thought, *Yeah, right. That woman probably never had school-age children!*

Then God softened my spirit as I considered for the first time that perhaps the problem was (*gasp!*) ME, not my son. Confessing my impatience and anger, I asked God for forgiveness. The next morning, I apologized to Jeff, too.

What did I learn from this process? When I lack virtue (which is just about all the time) and wisdom and faithful instruction fall between the slamming doors, God knows just how to short-circuit my undesirable motherly mechanisms!

Our Daughter Had Disappeared

ANITA HIGMAN

She said to herself, "If I only touch his cloak,
I will be healed."
Jesus turned and saw her.
"Take heart, daughter," he said,
"your faith has healed you."
And the woman was healed from that moment.
MATTHEW 9:21–22 NIV

Many years ago when my kids were little, my husband and I decided to treat them to a trip to a water park. The morning was as pretty as a bouquet of pastel balloons, and so we busied ourselves splashing around in our bathing suits.

Suddenly, my daughter Hillary—who was just beyond toddlerhood at the time—vanished. You have to know that I was one of those obnoxiously overprotective moms who barely let her kids sneeze without supervision. But nonetheless, our daughter had disappeared.

My husband, Peter, and I looked for our daughter, which turned into a heart-pounding, wild-eyed, frantic search.

In those seconds that felt like hours, I'm sure we thought of every scary scenario imaginable. And then we saw our daughter in the distance—cheerfully playing in one of the kiddy pools, unaware that she'd wandered off too far or that she was left vulnerable among strangers. She simply trusted us, as her parents, that we'd been watching over her comings and goings—that all was well.

One of the more fascinating passages in the Bible mentions not a lost child but a woman who had a peculiar illness. She'd suffered from an unnatural bleeding for many years. I can imagine her situation must have been miserable as well as embarrassing. But when that dear woman saw our Lord, she didn't beg Him for assistance but merely reached out to Him. Perhaps she was too embarrassed to state her ailment in front of a group of strangers. I would have been mortified. Perhaps that is why the woman followed through with her act of faith so quietly.

But what faith!

In her thoughts, which the Lord knew, she believed she only needed to touch His garment to be healed. If that scene were portrayed in a Mel Gibson movie, we would surely see a magnificent display of electricity coming through that garment to her body. But it wasn't special effects the woman was after, only healing. And she received it. Her faith made her whole.

Jesus healed countless people during His ministry on earth, and most of these personal stories were never mentioned in the Bible. Don't you wonder why this particular story was included? I can only guess that it was because her faith impressed God. Wow, I don't know about you, but *that* is the kind of faith I want!

How is my faith? After being a follower of Christ for decades, have I finally gotten to that place of childlike trust? I hope so, since I am that needy woman in the crowd. I pray I can always respond the way she did, never doubting His willingness to help me, never backing away into the crowd—away from His presence and touch. Instead, I want to always reach out my hand, my heart, and see that smile and hear those words, "Take heart, daughter, your faith has healed you."

A Few Firsts

DONNA K. MALTESE

*Have faith in God, who is rich
and blesses us with everything we need to enjoy life.*
1 TIMOTHY 6:17 CEV

Life is filled with firsts (first words, first steps, first day of school, etc.).

A few years ago, my son, Zach, then seventeen, and I experienced a few firsts. Zach had just obtained his permit, and I offered to teach him how to drive—a first for both of us. Before we left the house, I skimmed through PennDOT's tutor-tips booklet, taking to heart its words: *Stay calm, patient, and positive.*

With this mantra in my mind and a prayer on my lips, I drove to the church where I parked in the middle of the lot, turned off the car, and said to Zach, "Okay, let's switch places."

Once Zach was in the driver's seat, I began pointing out the car's controls, quizzing him on their functions. Some he was already familiar with; some needed explanation; and some, like the wipers, headlights, parking brake, horn, and turn signals, he gave a trial run. Next we reviewed the gears, as well as the pedals. After clicking on our seat belts, I told Zach to start the car—*just stay calm*—and, when ready, to shift into DRIVE.

After a few abrupt starts and stops, Zach proceeded to drive around the lot, stopping once in a while to park, at which time we'd both open up our car doors to see how close he'd gotten to the white lines. And so it went.

Twenty minutes later, somewhat dizzy from the circling tour of the somewhat small church lot, I proposed driving to the neighboring school. After making absolutely sure nothing was coming down the road, Zach pulled out onto Main Street and abruptly turned down the school road where he continued driving, parking, etc. At one point we spied a friend walking up the sidewalk. As Zach slowly passed her, I turned toward my window, gave her my impression of Edvard Munch's painting *The Scream*, and then faced forward again.

Zach, his eyes glued to the road, said, "Did you just give Mrs. K. some sort of horrified expression?"

"Uh, yeah."

"I thought so," he said, and smiled.

After our seemingly endless tour of the school grounds, I asked Zach if he was comfortable enough to drive into Perkasie where I'd buy him a treat to celebrate his first day of driving. He hesitated for only a second, then agreed, and we headed onto the public roads.

Just stay calm.

We eventually arrived at the bakery with Zach very

pleased and me very relieved.

Life is full of firsts, and on this particular foray into the unknown, I learned a few things: (1) no matter how many times I pump my foot, there is no actual brake pedal on the passenger side; (2) the ongoing mantra *"just stay calm"* can fly out of your head at a moment's notice; (3) sometimes blue pickup trucks appear closer than they actually are; (4) it pays to spend some one-on-one time with your kids—no matter how many gray hairs you accumulate in the process; and (5) to handle the sometimes nerve-racking firsts in life, we just need to have faith, stay calm, and endeavor to enjoy every moment!

Runaway!

JANICE HANNA

Where can I go from your Spirit?
Where can I flee from your presence?
PSALM 139:7 NIV

When my oldest daughter, Randi, was three, she was quite a handful. I'd never met a more precocious toddler. She was the sort to pitch a fit in public or throw a tantrum if she didn't get her way. I have to confess, there were times when I wondered why the Lord had sent me such a difficult child when others seemed to have such obedient little ones.

Randi was especially difficult at the grocery store. Her younger sister, Courtney (two years old), would sit in the front of the basket, and Randi would ride in the back with the goodies. This often turned out to be dangerous. For instance, cookies would get eaten, even before we paid for them at the register. Extra items would end up in the cart, things I never planned on purchasing. And often, when I'd turn away to grab merchandise from the shelf, Randi would sneak over the edge of the basket and take off running.

That's exactly what happened in the middle of a particularly lengthy shopping trip. Randi simply disappeared while my back was turned. I immediately went into a panic. I grabbed the shopping cart and took off sprinting down the aisle, making the turn at the end and glancing down the next aisle. Nothing. Then the next. No luck. And the next. Nada.

Finally, just about the time I thought I'd have to get the folks at customer service involved, a lady came strolling toward me with Randi at her side. They were holding hands, and my daughter had a sly smile on her face.

"Did you lose something?" the woman asked as she gave me one of those why-aren't-you-watching-your-kids-lady looks, and I shivered. I forced a smile and thanked her for returning my daughter, then lifted the naughty little girl back into the basket and continued on my way. Of course, I waited to scold Randi until after the woman who'd returned her to me was well out of earshot. Then I told the naughty youngster just how scared I'd been. I'll never forget her wide eyes and perfectly rounded mouth as she listened to my fear-induced tirade.

If you've ever lost one of your children—even for a minute or two—then perhaps you can relate to this story. There's nothing more terrifying than thinking you'll never see—or hold—your child again. Thankfully, our heavenly Father keeps a close eye on us. The Bible says that He knows our comings and our goings. We're never outside of His gaze. If we go to the depths, He meets us there. If we sail across the skies, He's right there, too. And just as I longed for my toddler to behave, He desires that we would do the things that please Him. Today, instead of sprinting from the basket and running from the Lord, turn and face Him. Leap into His arms. Settle into His loving embrace, and do all you can to be the obedient child He longs for you to be.

Mother, Mother on the Wall: Peace

Hiding Place

Renae Brumbaugh

You are my hiding place;
you will protect me from trouble and
surround me with songs of deliverance.

PSALM 32:7 NIV

Our conversation went something like this:

Me: Foster, are you excited about getting a betta fish?

Foster: Yes.

Me: What are you going to name your pet fish?

Foster: Jimmy. No, Sporty.

We had to go to three different places. The first store only sold reptiles—lots of slithery ones.

Foster: Can I have a pet snake instead of a fish?

Me: Get in the car. You're getting a fish.

The second store had everything we needed. Fish tanks, supplies, food, even a nice little bridge on which the fish could play. But no betta fish. We were invited to return in two weeks.

I bought the supplies, and we headed for the third place on our list. Bingo! Right when we walked in the door, we saw a row of betta fish, all lined up in their little cups. There were red ones, blue ones, black ones, and rainbow-colored ones.

Foster: I want a boy, no, girl fish.

Lady at the fish store: They're all boys.

Foster: Can I have two?

Lady at the fish store: You can't put two of them together in the same tank. They'll kill each other.

Foster: Cool! Can I have three?

I paid for one fish—yellow and white, with blue fins. Foster held the cup carefully as we got into the car.

Me: Be careful with Sporty. We don't want him to slosh too much on the way home.

Foster: His name isn't *Sporty*. It's *Goldie*.

Me: I thought it was *Sporty*.

Foster: That was before I saw him.

Made sense to me. We arrived home and placed Goldie on the kitchen counter. Foster lovingly poured the blue and green rocks in the bottom of the bowl, and then gently positioned the bridge so it wouldn't tip over. We placed some ivy in there, too, for decoration.

Finally, without much fanfare, we placed the cup in the bowl and set Goldie free. Sort of.

For the better part of the day, Foster kept his face pressed against the glass, watching Goldie's every move. Poor little fish. Must be pretty scary to have a six-year-old giant watching you around the clock. Before long, Goldie discovered that the ivy leaves made great hiding places.

Foster was both thrilled and frustrated with the

hide-and-seek game. Finally, he gave up and gave Goldie a break.

I can relate. Some days I need a place to hide. Sometimes, it feels like giants are watching. But during those times, I remember that I do have a Hiding Place. I have Someone I can run to, who has promised to hide me in the shadow of His wings. There, I feel safe.

Before bed, I asked Foster, "Did you feed Goldie?"

Foster: Mom, his name is *Jimmy*.

Pizza I Give You

JEAN FISCHER

Come, let us sing for joy to the LORD;
let us shout aloud to the Rock of our salvation.
PSALM 95:1 NIV

It wasn't that the Angeletti family didn't fit in, but more that they stood out in a church rich in the heritage of German Methodists. Mr. and Mrs. Angeletti and their six little Angelettis were Spirit-filled, born-again Christians, unusual for a family from Umbria, Italy. They spoke fluent English but with thick Italian accents, and. . .well. . .the Angeletti family was loud.

Mr. Angeletti—Salvatore—had a booming bass voice that contradicted his short stature and quiet personality. When he joined the church choir, our music director felt blessed. He had prayed for just such a voice for his group, made up mostly of tenors.

Perhaps the reason for Mr. Angeletti's quietness was that his wife liked to talk. When the family entered the vestibule on Sundays, you could hear Imelda Angeletti barking orders at her children and her husband, too.

"Salvatore! Watch little Giovanni so he don't fall-a down-a da stairs. Maria, spit out dat gum! Tomas! You be quiet in da church today."

Imelda enjoyed leading the mothers' Bible study group on Tuesdays, and on Sunday mornings she helped with children's church. Her forceful personality intimidated some of the children and even a few of the adults. Mrs. Angeletti could be warm and motherly, but when she quoted scripture and taught about Jesus, she was loud and dramatic.

One Sunday morning, Mrs. Angeletti taught a lesson about peace. As the children sat near the altar in a half circle around her, she read aloud from her Bible. "John 14:27. Peace-a I leave-a wit you; my peace-a I give-a to you. I do not give-a to you as da world gives. *Do not* let your hearts be troubled and *do not* be afraid."

To the children's and the congregation's surprise, Imelda followed her scripture reading with singing "Peace in the Valley," *a cappella*. Her strong alto voice belted out the well-known gospel song.

Afterward, a deafening silence filled the church. Mrs. Angeletti sat stone still, gazing prayerfully up toward heaven. When finally she lowered her head, she looked intently at the children seated around her. "*Blessed* are da peace-a-makers," she said. "For *dey* shall be known as da *children of God.* So?" she asked the little ones. "What-a you learn-a from today's lesson?"

One brave little boy spoke up. "You're going to give us pizza in the valley!"

"And God bless the pizza makers!" his sister added.

The mood in the church lightened. The worshippers laughed and Mrs. Angeletti did, too. "Praise God!" she shouted. "For da children!"

A verse in Job says, "God's voice thunders in marvelous ways." The same could be said about Imelda Angeletti. She was hard to understand sometimes. Her loud personality was intimidating, but her heart was in the right place. She loved God, and she wanted the whole world to know.

Wasp Wars

JEAN FISCHER

*You are my hiding place! You protect me from trouble,
and you put songs in my heart because you have saved me.*
PSALM 32:7 CEV

I remember my grandma on the hottest days of summer wearing sturdy rubber boots and hosing down her garden. She spent hours tending her flowers and vegetables. If a weed dared to poke through the well-tilled soil, Grandma attacked it with boiling water poured from the spout of an old metal teakettle.

Bugs crawled, flew, and skittered through Grandma's garden: brightly colored butterflies stretching on sunflowers, hoverflies dangling over zucchini blossoms, and at night, fireflies drifting through corn rows. I loved watching the bugs. They didn't bother me at all. But there was one kind that sent a jolt of fear from my head to my toes.

Wasps!

Early September days brought wasps. They sought the warmth of the concrete sidewalk that stretched from the front of our house to the side door. I remember sitting at my desk in elementary school watching the clock tick down to 3:15. My heart pounded as I imagined walking through the minefield of wasps. Sometimes I'd run up the sidewalk screaming, hoping that my cries would scare them away, praying that I wouldn't get stung. That worked until one day the angry wasps attacked, shoving their stingers into me three times. After that, I wouldn't walk on the sidewalk if I saw even one wasp. Instead, I stood out front until Grandma, or someone else, came to scare the wasps away.

One day while I was in school, the chrysanthemums bloomed. The hot Indian summer sunshine produced a sea of colorful flowers framing the dreaded sidewalk. Dozens of wasps, long legs dangling, flew to and fro. No way would I walk there! I stayed in the front yard determined to wait forever rather than face the pain of another wasp sting. Finally Grandma came to get me. Still, I refused to walk on that wasp-covered concrete.

"Stay there," Grandma said. "I have an idea."

She disappeared around the back of the house and returned with the garden hose. She turned it on full force and began belting the wasps with ice-cold blasts. As I stood, frozen with fear, Grandma held off the army of wasps with her water gun.

"Come on," she encouraged me. "You can do it!"

I hesitated.

Then Grandma started to sing:

"Onward, Christian soldiers, marching as to war,
with the cross of Jesus going on before.

Christ, the royal Master, leads against the foe;
forward into battle, see His banners go!"

Gathering all my courage, I raced up the sidewalk, trusting Grandma and God to protect me. They did. The wasps stayed away, and I didn't get stung.

Psalm 27:3 (NIV) says, "Though an army besiege me, my heart will not fear; though war break out against me, even then I will be confident." Today, when I encounter "wasps" on life's sidewalk, I think of that verse and of Grandma with her garden hose.

Unknown Territory

Donna K. Maltese

*"And surely I am with you always,
to the very end of the age."*
MATTHEW 28:20 NIV

In my eighth year, my parents sent me away from our summer bungalow to a camp deep in the woods of Finland, Pennsylvania. The minute I arrived with my pillow, red sleeping bag, and battered gray suitcase, I cried from homesickness. During cabin assignments, I cried. That night, lying in a strange bunk, I cried. Toward the middle of the week, I sat on a bee's nest. Counselors rushed me into the lodge and immediately applied wet mud to the injured area, an embarrassing and painful incident that turned out to be the highlight of my camp experience.

Each day I swam, ate lousy food, and gingerly sat down at craft tables to make works of art out of toothpicks, Popsicle sticks, and dried macaroni. Each night I cried myself to sleep.

Finally, the week was over! We packed our suitcases, rolled up our sleeping bags, and grabbed our pillows.

Today our parents were coming to pick us up! Oh, what joy! I imagined my mom rushing to me, lifting me up off the ground and into her arms, showering me with hugs and kisses, then taking me home, far away from this strange forest with unfamiliar paths.

One by one, parents came down that dirt road, their cars kicking up dust. One by one, each little girl was whisked up, tossed into a car, and driven home. I stood, my arms straining with the weight of my baggage. I looked over the heads of adults, trying to find a familiar face. The minutes passed. . .five, ten, fifteen.

I sat on my suitcase, a little more anxious but still excited. The sun set. And then there were two. Me and the last counselor. We sat there. We waited. No one came.

Finally the counselor asked, "Where do you live? Do you think you could find your way home?"

"I dunno," I sobbed.

She put me and my gear into her car. "It'll be all right, honey. We'll get you home."

Once we got out of the camp, the roads looked familiar. I'd only been a mile or two from our bungalow during the entire week!

Soon we were parked behind our little green cottage. The screen door slammed. My mother, shocked, ran to me, her arms out wide. "Oh, honey! I forgot to pick you up! Oh, I'm so, so sorry." She held me in her arms, my dirty, tear-streaked face pushed deep into her body. Stroking my hair, she soothed me until my tears were gone and only dry, shuddering sighs remained. How wonderful to be back home in Mom's arms.

I had never felt so scared as when I had been at camp, dropped in the middle of a strange forest with unfamiliar paths.

In life, every step we take is into unknown territory. But God is with us always. He'll keep us safe until we reach the end of our road, where He greets us with open arms.

(Oh, and moms. . .don't *ever* forget to pick your kids up from camp. Not only will it scar them for life, but you'll never hear the end of it.)

Prayers about Monsters

VALORIE QUESENBERRY

"Let the children come to me. Don't stop them!
For the Kingdom of God belongs to those who are like these children.
I tell you the truth, anyone who doesn't receive
the Kingdom of God like a child will never enter it."
Then he took the children in his arms and placed
his hands on their heads and blessed them.
MARK 10:14–16 NLT

In our family, my son holds the distinction of praying the funniest prayers. I wrote some of them down in his baby book, and they still make me smile when I read them.

Being a boy and having natural fears, his petitions to the Almighty were often for protection against monsters of one kind or another, most notably dinosaurs. He prayed that they wouldn't come in our "holes" (windows), that they wouldn't come into our house, and that they wouldn't get his baby sister.

To my adult ears, his prayers, though adorable, could have seemed unnecessary. I know there aren't dinosaurs in existence today, so he didn't need to pray for protection from them. In other words, from a purely adult point of view, his prayers were pointless.

But that's missing the focus of prayer.

Our Father tells us to pray to Him, not about what He knows, but about what we fear. From His perspective, every single one of our fears could seem silly. He knows that He is not going to let anything get close to us that is outside of His will. He knows we have no need to pray for protection from the "monsters" that lurk in our minds.

Yet He tells us to pray anyway. Just as He welcomed the little children to come to Him with their childish ways, so He welcomes us with our incomplete knowledge and earthly concerns.

I'm a mom to my kids, but to my heavenly Father, I'm still a child. I still need to know that I can approach Him and be welcomed. I still need the reassurance that He won't turn me away because He is too busy with the "big" people. I still need to know that He has time for a "kid" like me. I still need His blessing on a regular basis.

Like my son, I have fears. I fear world disasters and political unrest. I fear inevitable disease and death in my family. I fear the unknown events of the future. I fear for my children's health, their personal safety, their future spouse, their spiritual development, their adult decisions, and the list goes on. And I can bring those fears to Him in complete confidence that He will not turn me away. He understands the "monsters" that I see. My limited perspective does not irritate or frustrate Him. He listens to my fears and gives me grace out of His vast storehouse.

To me, there is nothing sweeter than a child's voice lifted in prayer. No matter what he asks for, I cherish the simple faith that precipitates the request. And I imagine that's the way it is with us as God's children. He looks past the words to the heart. And He rewards a childlike approach with His Fatherly care. I'm sure glad, because no matter how "grown up" I am, I'll still need it.

Explosion!

JANICE HANNA

"In your anger do not sin":
Do not let the sun go down while you are still angry.
EPHESIANS 4:26 NIV

While preparing breakfast for my family one morning, I placed an unopened can of biscuits on the counter and then left the room to tend to something else. Suddenly I heard a terrible explosion. It sounded like a gunshot or possibly a sonic boom. I raced to the kitchen, my heart thumping madly! What had happened?

Imagine my surprise when I discovered that biscuits covered the entire room. There were biscuits on the wall, biscuits on the counter, and biscuits on the floor. I'd never seen anything like it. The pressure inside the can had obviously built to a point where the explosion occurred. And what a mess! My husband and children joined me seconds later, their eyes—and mouths—wide. None of us dared move until we were sure the explosion had fully ended. Then the laughter started. (Well, until I asked them to help me clean up the gooey blobs of dough anyway! Then their laughter turned to groaning.)

It took us quite awhile—working together—to clean up the mess. If you've ever handled warm dough, you know how sticky it can be! And it doesn't smell great either! Oh, and getting up to the ceiling to scrub it off? Well, that was something I'd never planned for! Neither had I planned for the blob that fell into my hair as I worked. Disgusting!

Can you relate to that kind of explosion? Most of us who have kids can! We let our frustrations build, and—*wham*—something triggers an explosion. Biscuits come shooting out of the can. We make a tremendous amount of noise and mess up everything in sight. We leave a shocked audience—often our children—to clean up after us. And we feel like crawling into a hole afterward, because we're so ashamed of our behavior. This is not the kind of parent we'd planned to be, is it? But what else can we do about it? Parenting is hard work, filled with unexpected challenges. Tempers often reach the boiling point—and not always when we expect it!

How do we stop anger? It must be diffused at its root. Oh sure, we do our best to tuck frustrations with our children away into the secret places, thinking we've got everything under control, but we often fall short. The proof is in the pudding, as my mama used to say. If we live as servants, as Christ instructed, there is no room left for the kind of anger that lashes out or hurts others, especially our own kids. Sure, there will be plenty of opportunities to forget, but we have to make a conscious effort not to let the pressure build to the danger point.

Otherwise, those biscuits will mess up a perfectly lovely room (and a perfectly lovely family).

Today, spend some time bowing your knee, asking God to show you how to deal with frustrations His way! He wants those biscuits in the can, where they belong!

Send in the Clown

S. A. FULLER

All Scripture is God-breathed and is useful for teaching,
rebuking, correcting and training in righteousness,
so that the servant of God may be thoroughly
equipped for every good work.
2 TIMOTHY 3:16–17 NIV

One television show that Mom and I never missed was a locally produced, half-hour variety show called *Bozo the Clown*. Every Wednesday afternoon with magic and skits about friendship, sharing, and compassion, Bozo taught and entertained while interacting with an audience of middle schoolers. A lucky few were called on stage to be a part of his act.

It was a big deal when we got the news that my sixth-grade class would be featured on the show. We had to wait three long weeks before the scheduled taping. Mom took advantage of the time lapse to keep me on my best behavior. Any infraction and she'd riddle me this: "Guess who won't be meeting Bozo?"

Between threats that my class would be going to the

show without me, she'd warn me that I'd face corporal punishment if I wandered away from the group during the trip or didn't mind my teachers. It wasn't until the morning she escorted me to the bus we were taking that she lightened up. She hugged me tight and said, "Have fun."

Overcome by nerves and anticipation, we rode in silence to Bozo's studio. Only Mrs. Graham and her aide, Mrs. Gibbons, were relaxed enough to chat about the weather, other teachers, and their roles in securing our coveted appearance.

As soon as we arrived, Bozo's staff hustled us onto the set, lined us up, and hatched out a seating plan. I was the tallest person in our class and was quickly escorted to the back row. My vertically challenged classmates were shuffled around more times than a scrambled Rubik's Cube.

Once they were satisfied with where everyone was sitting, the staff disappeared. We spent the rest of the morning glued to rock-hard bleachers, waiting for Bozo. Lunchtime whizzed by. We began to realize that celebrity had its price.

We spotted Bozo in his usual long-sleeved, polka-dot jumpsuit with round, ruffled collar, white gloves, and matte white face paint. A red, cherry-sized bubble covered the tip of his nose, and a bushy, powdered Afro quadrupled his head size. He looked us over without fully acknowledging our squeals and waves.

The next time we saw him, he was eating a powdered doughnut and drinking a cup of coffee. By then, most of us were more interested in sharing his snack than his comedic antics.

The final time he made an appearance, the cameras were rolling. His performance was flavored with gag props and quirky sound effects that appeared as mysteriously as UFOs from his sleeves or secret compartments in his clown suit. The taping ended too soon. We were tired and hungry but willing to stay all night to scream affirmations to Bozo's constant queries (per instruction) and see the tricks he had in store.

"Stealing is wrong. Right, kids?"

"Right, Bozo."

"We should always tell the truth. Right, kids?"

"Right, Bozo."

The two-hour ride home was loud and chaotic as all of us tried to tell each other about things we'd seen and to hear about anything we thought we'd missed.

Later, when Mom and I watched the show, we giggled at everything, both of us glad that we'd share the memory of my day with Bozo forever.

SECTION 8

COOL MOMS WEAR JELLY: GRACE

Clinging to the Nest

TINA KRAUSE

There the birds make their nests.
PSALM 104:17 NIV

When my firstborn graduated from high school, I was traumatized. Anticipating Jimmy's departure for college was as foreboding as sitting in a dentist's chair braced for a tooth extraction. And—I might add—just as painful.

One Sunday morning our minister summoned the graduates and their parents to the front of the church. Knowing I'd need it, I grabbed a wad of tissue before joining the others on the platform.

After the pastor prayed and issued congratulations, we filed back to our pews. Attempting to withhold my sobs, I pressed the tissue against my quivering lips. But just before I reached my seat, an elderly gray-haired lady reached out to grab my sleeve. "Don't worry," she whispered with a sheepish grin, "he'll be back."

Her words, like my offspring, have returned to haunt me ever since. Both sons returned home, causing me to wonder if my emotional brouhaha was simply a case of temporary insanity.

It seems today's return-to-the-roost chicks cling to the nest with both claws. Take Bill for example—a bright, responsible, twenty-five-year-old man. I sat beside him on a flight to Chicago. He was an accounting major, employed by a large financial firm.

"So, do you live close to your parents?" I probed, having talked with him for a while. He grinned. "Yeah, I live real close. I live with them." I then spouted words I vowed I'd never say. "You know, in my day we left home as soon as possible."

Bill was visibly thrilled. He was seated next to a middle-aged Chatty Cathy with the curiosity of the paparazzi and the chutzpah of a Jewish matchmaker.

Undaunted, I asked Bill why he preferred the nest. "It's easier and more comfortable at home," he admitted. "My mom launders my clothes and cooks all my meals." Bill's confession struck me like the snap of a wet towel: it explained why my own capable twenty-something sons kept migrating home.

How unpredictably the tide turns. When our sons were born, my husband and I devised a plan. After college they'd secure a great job, marry a nice girl, and raise 2.5 adorable children who would visit their grandparents once a week. Of course, parental plans seldom actualize, so we fashioned Plan B: After they vacate, we'll sell the house, move to another state, and forget to leave a forwarding address.

We love our sons, but there comes a time when one nest no longer accommodates four adults. Somehow the pitter-patter of men's sizes 11 and 13 feet doesn't make me want to peruse *Parents* magazine anymore. Rather, after stumbling over my sons' shoes and picking up their dirty laundry, I shriek, "Hey, when will you guys get a life?" All the while I wipe my tears with a wad of tissue and search for that wise, gray-haired lady, hoping this time she'll have better news.

Note from the author: Today, both sons and their families reside in secure nests of their own!

Unusual Sleep Habits

Rachel Quillin

And he was in the hinder part of the ship,
asleep on a pillow: and they awake him, and say unto him,
Master, carest thou not that we perish?
Mark 4:38 KJV

The phrase "sleeping like a baby" is highly overrated, at least in a positive sense. It's true that as a mom I have slept pretty much just like each of my babies, which means that during much of their infancy I was exhausted. Very few of my children actually slept through the night prior to their first birthdays. It was all fine for them. They could nap anytime they felt tired. That was not so much the case from my perspective.

However, as my kids have grown, their sleep patterns have gradually become more bearable and at times even entertaining. How many times have you watched a small child in a high chair struggling to keep his eyes open and finally succumbing to fatigue, spoon in mouth or half-eaten sandwich in hand? It's a classic photo op. The camera comes out, and everyone laughs about it being a great picture to put up at the poor child's high school graduation party. Then someone dutifully whisks the little guy off to more comfortable sleeping quarters—sans the spoon or sandwich, of course.

Small children generally do not worry much about the panic attacks they create for their parents when they disappear at any given time for a nap. Such was the case as I prepared a meal one day. My children were happily playing outside when suddenly the smallest was gone. I went all around the yard looking for him and calling for him. My greatest fear was that he had wandered into the woods. Before calling my husband, I decided to look in the house. I hadn't seen the little guy come in, but there was always that chance. Good thing I looked. He was sound asleep in his bed. Turns out he can be pretty quiet and sneaky when he wants to be. Even now he can be hiding right in front of me, and I will miss him.

On another occasion, I was preparing to leave the kids with a babysitter. I wanted to make sure all was in order and that each child was accounted for. One was missing. I looked in the kids' newest favorite place to play, and there she was, contentedly napping under the bed. Really now, I'm pretty sure it would not have been terribly complicated to crawl out from under the bed and onto the mattress, but she had a different idea. Try explaining that to a babysitter!

Then we come to child five, who does things his own way. For the longest time he would throw stuffed animals on the floor and demand his baseball, basketball, soccer ball. . .you get the point. And of course when he got a new pair of gum boots, he had to wear those to bed, too.

You know, young children sleep in many strange ways, and a lot of adults don't sleep at all. Kids enjoy life. Adults worry too much. Our focus is on things outside of our control rather than on the One who controls everything. Isn't it time to shift our focus?

Two and Already Showing Her Training

PATRICIA GRAU

Start children off on the way they should go,
and even when they are old they will not turn from it.
PROVERBS 22:6 NIV

As an American married to a German, I wanted my daughter to blend easily with her family from both countries. Since my husband's family spoke German and mine spoke English, we reasoned that Lila would need to learn both languages.

Although my parents had never said anything, I knew they had doubts about our decision to begin Lila's bilingual training at birth. After researching the language learning process, my husband and I were confident she could simultaneously learn both languages. I spoke and read to Lila in English. Her papa used German. When Lila began to talk, we were pleased with her ability to use English and German words. She seemed to follow our lead and normally didn't mix the two languages.

As I packed for our annual family visit to the States, I anticipated the joy my parents would have seeing Lila.

Although I admit it was vain, I hoped they would be impressed by her and, therefore, my abilities as a mom. Not only was she starting to talk, in my opinion she was very well behaved.

Luckily I had yet to see any signs of the dreaded terrible twos. I didn't know when she would start to show her temper with little tantrums. However, my parenting book assured me that tantrums were not optional. It was just a matter of time before she would begin testing her will. Hopefully, we could get back home before she felt the need to assert herself with tantrums.

I couldn't have been happier with our visit. Grandpa and Grandma were charmed by their youngest grandchild. My mother even commented that we were doing a good job training Lila. I proudly added that, so far, she hadn't displayed any terrible-twos behavior.

My mother just smiled at my declaration.

On the last day of our visit, I put Lila in the high chair as we prepared for lunch. It took another ten minutes before everyone was seated. By then, Lila was drumming up quite a ruckus on the wooden tray of the high chair. I asked her to stop banging her spoon. She ignored me, so I repeated myself. She seemed to escalate the banging, until my husband turned to her and commanded in German, "Lila, stop banging your spoon."

Lila glared at her papa and yelled, "Nein, nein, nein!" She immediately turned to me, banged her spoon again, and yelled, "No, no, no!" Stunned, I sat mute as my husband took the spoon away from Lila.

When I glanced at my mother, she smiled as she started passing food. "Somebody's terrible twos have arrived. It seems like you've trained her up in the way she should go, and as a two-year-old, she's going to bless you with tantrums in both German and English."

Being Candid with God

Marcia Hornok

I cry out to the LORD with my voice. . . .
I pour out my complaint before Him;
I declare before Him my trouble.
PSALM 142:1–2 NKJV

In the early seventies, when breastfeeding was uncommon, I was the only mom in my circle of friends who chose to do it. My friends' children were often curious when they saw me nursing Jesse. One child asked her mother, "When Mrs. Hornok has Jesse under the blanket like that, is she milking him?"

Another time, a four-year-old asked me what I was doing to my baby. I said, "I'm feeding him milk."

She thought about that—then asked, "And crackers?"

Children often express themselves candidly, unaware of taboos or inhibitions. We laugh at their innocent observations, like when my three-year-old son, Nathan, announced one morning, "Everybody's bottom is in the back." This may have been prompted by having a new baby in the house. He probably noticed a universal truth about bottoms while watching me bathe his sister, Esther.

However, I was not prepared for his candid remark one evening when we had guests for dinner. As we were all sitting around the table, Nathan suddenly asked, "How did Esther get out of your tummy?" I answered briefly and quickly, enough to keep him from asking more questions.

A few days later, I learned my explanation had made an impression on him. As he watched me squeeze vitamin drops into Esther's mouth, he said, "God makes a special hole for vitamins."

Yes, children innocently speak what's on their mind, whether appropriate or not. By the same token, God invites His children to speak to Him at any time about any topic. Nothing is off-limits. The psalm writers often questioned God about how long He was taking to answer them or why He was hiding His face. Job called on God to defend Himself. In chapter ten, he freely complained to God and spoke in the bitterness of his soul.

Although we cannot figure out our infinite Father or understand all His dealings with us, He allows us to say what's on our mind. Raising children provides many occasions for that. We can run to Him with our needs, questions, sorrows, and fears, as well as with our joys and gratitude. We have the phenomenal privilege to be open and candid with God.

The psalm that begins with crying out to the Lord with complaints and troubles ends with this certainty: "You shall deal bountifully with me" (142:7). God will parent us as we parent the little ones He has entrusted to us.

The Great Escape

DONNA K. MALTESE

But God demonstrates His own love toward us,
in that while we were still sinners, Christ died for us.
ROMANS 5:8 NKJV

When my sisters and I were growing up, we had a common toy called a paddleball. This consisted of an elastic string stapled to a flat wooden paddle. At the other end of the string was a small, red, rubber ball. The trick was to see how many times you could hit the ball with the paddle without missing. Over the years, my sisters and I went through a number of these paddleballs since they were not very durable playthings.

Also, when we were kids, parents spanking their children was the norm. The tool my parents used in this mode of punishment was a broken paddleball paddle. When this wood hit the backside, it stung more than it stunned, but it still managed to get the point across.

One of these broken toy paddles was kept in the top drawer of the tall dresser, which my sisters and I couldn't reach. We'd always known we'd gone too far when, after some infraction on our part, my parents instructed us to stay where we were while they went upstairs and into that drawer to retrieve the infamous implement of parental wrath.

One day, my sister Joann, the middle child, had done something that, in my mom's mind, deserved a spanking. She instructed Joann to stay where she was, then headed upstairs to retrieve the paddle. But this time, when Mom came downstairs with the tool in hand, Joann decided to make a run for it. In her great escape, she flew down the basement steps, with Mom hard on her trail. In her panic, Joann raced by the couch, then began running around a perfectly round antique table near the bay window. Mom began chasing her, and together they went around and around the table. Joann was determined not to get caught. On the other hand, Mom was determined to catch her. Both of them began panting in their exertions, yet each pressed on, doggedly resolute to win the race. Several minutes of this inane chase scene continued until both Jo and Mom realized the ridiculousness of the situation and fell to the floor, laughing hysterically.

That particular day, Joann escaped her punishment. Other days she wasn't so fortunate. Of course, as we grew older, the paddle was put away for good and our punishment took different forms, such as being grounded or having TV-watching or phone privileges taken away.

Now, as moms ourselves, my sisters and I invoke punishments—groundings or loss of TV or cell phone privileges—on our own children, and although they never take the form of spanking, they also manage to get our point across.

How wonderful that Jesus' sacrifice has taken the punishment we deserve for our misdeeds. Because of His death on the cross, we are freed from sin. Now that's a great escape!

The Look

JANICE HANNA

"The LORD lift up His countenance on you,
and give you peace."
NUMBERS 6:26 NASB

Every mother on planet earth knows how to give "the look" when she's upset with her kids. Oh, c'mon. . .you know the one. The eyes narrow. Every muscle in your face grows tight. You could bore holes through metal with your glare. The lips are pursed so tightly they look like prunes. You speak a thousand words without ever saying a thing.

The look. There's no school to educate young mothers on how to give it. There's no training manual on the subject, and you won't find any "How to Give the Look" articles in parenting magazines. It's one of those "tricks of the trade" that comes naturally to mothers, usually making its first appearance about the time a child reaches the toddler stage. And by the time kids are in their teens, mothers are experts at it.

When my girls were young, I became quite skilled at

giving "the look," especially when the kids misbehaved in public—which happened a lot. The oh-no-you-don't look came in handy, conveying every emotion I'd kept bottled up in one single glance: If you don't stop acting like that immediately, there will be serious consequences when we get home. If you even think about smarting off to me, there will be a price to pay. Stop it now before I intervene. I brought you into this world. . . I can take you out. Oh, how I excelled at conveying so many emotions in one penetrating look. Who knew I had this skill?

The look. Every child shivers in fear at the thought of it, and most line up and walk in a straight line after witnessing it. Those who don't are destined to see it again. . . and again.

God has a "look," too, but His is considerably different from the one that we moms give our kids. Even when we're on our worst behavior, He looks at us with nothing but love pouring from His eyes. We know we're safe to approach Him, even when we've misbehaved. He won't knee-jerk or bend us over His knee. Sure, there will be consequences to follow our poor actions, but He doesn't administer them with His face tightened in anger. When we come into His presence and gaze into His love-filled eyes, His "look" shows us everything we'd ever want to know in a glance—the error of our ways, the pain we've caused Him, our need for repentance, and so on. Our heavenly Father doesn't threaten or cajole when we've been naughty. Instead, He extends His hand and whispers, "Come here, my child. Sit in my lap. Let's spend some time together and get past this." Oh, what a precious invitation! What an opportunity to get to know Him more.

Rush into His arms today and look upon that glorious face. Memorize "the look" so that you can share it with your children when they're in need of grace and forgiveness.

The Garage Doors

Janice Hanna

"But as for you, you meant evil against me;
but God meant it for good, in order to bring it
about as it is this day, to save many people alive."
GENESIS 50:20 NKJV

In the mid-1990s we had the honor and privilege of opening our home to an "adopted" daughter, Courtney. She came from a troubled home and needed a safe place to stay, one where she would be loved unconditionally. I had an opportunity to extend unconditional love the summer she turned sixteen.

Because I worked from home when my girls were in their teens, I was often distracted. Such was the case on this day. I was in my home office, buried in work, when my third-oldest daughter, Megan, came in to tell me she needed to shift the vehicles in the driveway to get her car out. I handed her my keys and went back to work, fighting that nagging feeling that I'd somehow made a mistake in handing over those keys. A short time later I thought I heard a strange noise but didn't really think anything of it when the house grew silent again. Only when Megan and Courtney came tearing into my office screaming did I realize something had really happened.

I could hardly make sense of their words. Something about Courtney getting behind the wheel of my van. Something about her accidentally putting the car into DRIVE when she meant to put it in REVERSE. Something about her driving through the closed garage door and destroying much of the furniture in the garage that I'd been storing for a friend. Something about the condition of my van. The story was told so fast—and in so many choppy, tear-filled bits—that I could barely make sense of it. Surely I'd misunderstood.

And then I looked into Courtney's eyes—filled with terror. Nope. I hadn't misunderstood.

I ran straight outside to check out the damage. Except for a few bumps and bruises, the van appeared in pretty good shape. The garage door, on the other hand, was shot. And so was my friend's desk, which had been sitting just inside the door. Not that I really cared about these items of course. The girls' safety was foremost in my mind. At least, thank God, no one had been hurt. Things could be replaced. My children could not.

I stared at the mess and shrugged, opting not to offer any sort of punishment at all, short of a little lecture about how Courtney should've waited until she had her license to drive. Megan then confessed that she'd asked Courtney to help her out by moving one car while she moved the other.

Ultimately, we got new garage doors. They were a huge

step up from the old ones. Best of all, insurance paid for the whole thing. Who would have known the Lord could take a situation like that and turn it around, for both our good and His glory?

The next time you're in the middle of a situation that seems really bad, take a deep breath and wait. God will surely turn it around and use it for His glory. And while you're at it, why not praise Him in the midst of your circumstances?

Unbranded

JANICE HANNA

But if we confess our sins to him,
he is faithful and just to forgive us our sins
and to cleanse us from all wickedness.
1 JOHN 1:9 NLT

I'd been away for the weekend at a wonderful Christian retreat center. Oh, what a glorious, peaceful time I'd had, seeking the Lord and praying for His will and purpose in my life. When I arrived home, my four daughters—all teens and early twenty-somethings—had already left for a Christian concert. I planned to join them later. I walked through the house, bags in hand, and stopped short when I saw the kitchen table. Something about it looked different. . .but what?

I stared at it for a moment before something registered. It was beautifully decorated. Placemats. Plates. Cups. Silverware. All the works.

"Wow." I stared at the table, mesmerized by its beauty.

After a few seconds, however, I got that irritating feeling that moms often get. Suspicion set in. Why would the girls have done this? We weren't expecting company. And they'd gone to great detail. It was almost like they were covering up something.

Covering something up?

The idea took root. . .and all the more as I noticed an unusual spot on the table under the edge of one of the placemats. Just as I reached to take a closer look, I noticed a folded note on the plate. I picked it up and read it. "Dear Mom," my youngest daughter had written, "I ruined the dining room table by using it as an ironing board."

At once I pulled back the placemat, gasping as I saw the perfect imprint of an iron burned into my beautiful oak table. "No!" I thought about several things at once—how much I'd paid for the table just a few months prior. How I loved to entertain guests. How silly my daughter had been for not using a real ironing board. Oh! Just wait till I saw her face-to-face! She'd get a piece of my mind, for sure!

I rushed out the front door and drove to the concert to meet my girls. On the way there, the Lord very clearly spoke to my heart, instructing me to offer grace to my daughter. And when I saw her tear-filled eyes. . .when I heard the story of what she'd been through. . .when I heard the profuse apologies. . .how could I do anything else but forgive her?

Several years after the table was branded, I passed it on to my oldest daughter. Her breakfast room was small enough that she felt led to remove the center leaf in the table. Ironically, most of the imprint was on that leaf. So when I look at the table now, I don't see an iron mark—I see a beautiful round table, perfectly placed in a sun-filled breakfast room.

Isn't that just how we feel when we sin? We feel we're branded by what we've done. We allow it to define us. However, God wants to lift it from us, in much the same way that center leaf was lifted out of my dining room table. When we're forgiven, the Lord removes our sin from us—as far as the east is from the west. He wants us to extend forgiveness to others when they've hurt us, too. If you've "branded" others (friends, family members, or even yourself), why not choose to extend forgiveness today?

SECTION 9

"MIGHTY MOM" AND OTHER MYTHS: CONTENTMENT

Growing Up with Our Kids

ARDYTHE KOLB

When I was a child, I spoke as a child,
I understood as a child, I thought as a child;
but when I became a man, I put away childish things.
1 CORINTHIANS 13:11 NKJV

I was only twenty when our first baby was born, and it took less than a day to realize I was totally unprepared for this venture. My husband was in the navy, stationed on Guam, and I lived with my parents in Kansas City. When Jerry arrived home, he expected his baby to automatically love him. But Debbie saw no reason to add a daddy to her little circle of friends. Fortunately her initial rejection didn't permanently damage their relationship.

The only way to gain experience is through practice, so we added four more children, which helped us become more knowledgeable. And God probably said, "What have I allowed?" But He protected the kids from our ignorance.

Young parents do things mature parents wouldn't consider. One hot summer we were building an addition to our house. Our children were joined by neighborhood friends when a cement truck came to pour the driveway. Jerry said, "Go ask your parents if you can help settle the rocks." What child doesn't want to play in wet concrete? When the job was finished, we hosed them off and they ran home, bubbling with excitement.

In the midst of the same project, our three sons, aged eight, six, and four, climbed up on the roof to help Daddy with shingles. No doubt experienced parents would have considered the danger. To us it was an adventure. Extra angels must have been on duty that day.

Years later I should have had better mothering skills but definitely qualified for the "Dumb Mum" award when our son had appendicitis. After I came home from work, Erik complained of a stomachache. He was growing fast and was sometimes just too busy to eat right. I said, "What have you eaten today?"

"Not much. I didn't feel good."

"I'm fixing spaghetti. That'll help."

He downed dinner, but within an hour he said, "I still feel sick."

"How about a Tums?"

He complied. However, before long he said, "Mom, I think you should call the doctor."

When a fourteen-year-old says that, you pay attention. I felt his forehead and asked, "Where, exactly, do you hurt?"

He pointed to his right side. I checked his temperature, but it was normal. However, we did call the doctor and took Erik to the emergency room. By then his temp had risen several degrees. The nurse gave me a withering look.

"I really can read a thermometer," I defended myself.

They wheeled Erik into surgery to remove his appendix while I wrestled with my inadequacies as a mother.

Scripture encourages us to put away childish things, and with God's help we do. In the meantime, we learn to trust His loving care even when we behave like foolish children.

Dipstick!

TINA KRAUSE

Sin is not ended by multiplying words,
but the prudent hold their tongues.
PROVERBS 10:19 NIV

While raising our two sons, my husband and I tried to not make inappropriate comments that were less than Christian. Name-calling was taboo, and we were intolerant of the use of rude phrases such as "Shut up" or "You're stupid." So you can imagine my teenage sons' surprise when they heard me call someone a name for the first time in their adolescent lives.

As I drove the boys somewhere that eludes me now, another car careened in front of us, forcing me to slam on the brakes and swerve to the side of the road. Instantly the word popped out of my mouth faster than Jack springs out of his box.

"Dipstick!" I barked, as the driver zoomed ahead.

"Did you hear that, Jeff?" son Jimmy rallied from the backseat. "Mom called that guy a *dipstick!*"

"Wow, Mom," Jeff chimed in. "That was great! [hearty

guffaws] I can't believe you called that guy a name!"

You would have thought that I uttered my first recognizable word. The jovial twosome was more enthusiastic and delighted than if I had just given them permission to take a week off school to do nothing but play computer games.

It was time to tone them down. "I know, guys," I said in my most maternal let's-be-sensible tone. "I shouldn't have said that. I was wrong," I admitted, attempting to counter their gleeful satisfaction while underscoring a moral lesson through confession all at the same time. "Name-calling is never justified," I stated with conviction.

But no go. They ignored my contrition as their verbal elation continued. "Man, how cool was that!" Jimmy exclaimed.

"Yeah, Mom. I never heard you call anyone a *dipstick* before!" Jeff added as they bounded back and forth recounting my blunder, *ad nauseam*.

The only thing left to do was to wave the white flag. "That's right—I called that guy a *dipstick*, okay? Do you mind? It happened, so let's just let it go if that's all right with you!" I spouted.

My protest only supplied them with more fodder for the pigsty, and to this day I still hear about that hilarious moment when Mom lost it in a spontaneous burst of unrestrained anger. All of the sound words of wisdom I had spoken over the years disappeared in the fog of one incident that sparked their interest with intrinsic folly.

Finally my son Jimmy noticed my frustration. "Hey,

Mom," he said, "it's okay—you're only human."

Witnessing my outburst made my sons feel better about themselves because it confirmed to them what I had known all along—Mom is less than perfect. Way less. After all, how many times had I thought, *idiot!* or *jerk!* but just didn't vocalize it? Well, let's not go there. I'm still trying to live down *dipstick*.

A Strange and Impossible Notion

ANITA HIGMAN

"As for God, his way is perfect:
The LORD's word is flawless."
2 SAMUEL 22:31 NIV

Somewhere in the early stages of my children's lives I got the strange and impossible notion that I could be a super mom. Whoever put that idea into my head needs a reality check—or perhaps the gentle influence of a petite hammer on his or her toe! In fact, any woman who's even considered taking on that persona should pause, breathe deeply, and consider this—it's as easy to be a super mom as it is for Superman to fly in real life.

By now, you're primed for some juicy details on how I failed at this unattainable goal. You see, I not only aspired to be a perfect mom to my children, but I aspired to be perfect in every aspect of their lives. I'll only mention one here—their health. I'd grown up watching Jack LaLanne on TV, and so I thought my kids should be a little like him: trim, healthy, and full of energy. So, I fed my children superhealthy foods, like tofu pumpkin pie, raw fruits and veggies, natural peanut butter, and even seaweed for snacks! You get the picture.

But living that way didn't always work. Just to give you an example, one day my son, Scott, who could be quite the tattletale, yelled for me to come and see what he'd found under the couch. When I got there and lifted the fabric, I discovered a pile of children's chewable vitamins. My daughter, who was just a little gal at the time, had only been pretending to take her vitamins. Instead of gobbling them up, she'd been making a tidy little mound of them under the furniture. I should have taken that as a sign. I should have ripped off my Super Mom suit right there and hid it under the couch along with those nasty-tasting vitamins. But instead, over time, I learned to make some reasonable compromises here and there so that everyone in our family could live happily as well as healthily.

While my humanity showed through my Super Mom suit time and time again, I found God up for the task. He was then, and still is, the all-knowing, almighty One who has flawless parenting skills. His way is indeed perfect. He can be counted on to take care of my family in every area of our lives. He will love and cherish us, watch out for us, give us good gifts, discipline us, encourage us, inspire us, and bandage our wounds when we fall down.

I love my kids. I always will. They are my treasures. In fact, it's hard not to think of them all grown up now without my hand going to my heart. Or without getting a little misty eyed. But even with all that affection and devotion, from time to time I still fail as a mom. And when I do, I pray they will always remember this great truth: in Him we really should and *can* trust.

Those Two Precious Words

ANITA HIGMAN

Jesus asked, "Were not all ten cleansed?
Where are the other nine? Has no one returned
to give praise to God except this foreigner?"
LUKE 17:17–18 NIV

When my kids were little, my husband and I didn't expect to hear a lot of gratitude for all the caring attention we showered on them, and that was just fine. We were just thrilled to be their parents. But if you're a mom, you know what I'm writing about: all the times I cooked hot meals—thousands of them—all the times I watched that potty-training video, the emergency times when I tried not to pass out from all the blood, the scrubbing-of-the-couch-cushion-from-all-the-throwing-up times, the math-homework-that-made-Mom-feel-really-stupid times, and of course, the crawling-into-bed-with-us-during-those-bad-dreams times.

But now fast-forward many years. My son, Scott, was in college and was at home sick with a stomach virus. I stayed with him through it all, with each round of illness and cleanup, offering him whatever I could think of that might ease his suffering. He gradually recovered, and when he was finally feeling human again, he said a genuine, "Thanks, Mom." He didn't send me a thank-you card or get Robert Frost–like about his appreciation, but those two precious words truly warmed my heart.

Scott's grateful spirit and my appreciation of it remind me of that passage in the Bible when Jesus heals the ten men who suffered from leprosy. Jesus was going into a village, and the lepers called out, "Master, have pity on us!" And if you know the story, you know that Jesus did have mercy on them. He instructed them to show themselves to the priests. As they followed through with what Jesus said, they were healed of their disease.

But one man was so filled with thankfulness, he came back to thank Jesus. He didn't just say, "Thank You." The man returned giving praise to God, and he said it with a shout! The man went beyond words and threw himself down at the feet of Jesus. This is certainly the portrait of a man who has a grateful heart.

Jesus not only appreciated the man's return, but He asked why the other nine had not come back to praise God as well.

Makes me wonder. How is it between God and me when it comes to gratitude? Have I said those two precious words to my Savior today? Do I remember to acknowledge Him for His answered prayers? His daily presence and provision? His promise that I will spend eternity with Him?

How many times have I denied Jesus my grateful heart? Those times I've taken His life gifts and eternal promises, and I've hurried away like the nine healed lepers? Perhaps I've been guilty of forgetting to even look back at Him with a smile.

When I've absentmindedly held back my appreciation, I'm so glad that I can make it right again. I can open up my arms to the heavens and shout His glory. I can run to Him with praise and thanksgiving!

The Biscuit Brigade

JANET ROCKEY

*"Man does not live by bread alone,
but man lives by everything that proceeds
out of the mouth of the LORD."*
DEUTERONOMY 8:3 NASB

Mother thwacked the biscuit canister on the edge of the counter. The dough oozed from the ruptured can. She plopped the prefab biscuits into a cake pan and slid them into the oven.

I was fourteen and watched from the kitchen door. "Mother, why don't you make biscuits from scratch like Grandmother?"

A shadow crossed her face, telling me some questions are better left unasked.

"No one can make her biscuits," Mother answered, leveling a sad gaze at me. "No one."

"But you sew as well as she does," I argued on her behalf. "And you knit, too."

Mother handed the flatware to me. "Some qualities are passed down from one generation to the next. Some aren't."

"But—"

"Set the table, please."

My rebuttal had ended.

My older sister, Kathy, set the plates between the knives and forks. "Even Aunt Mackie can't make them," she whispered.

Later that summer, Grandmother Mary Belle came to visit from Texas.

Dad put her luggage in the den, while Mother, Kathy, and I surrounded Mary Belle, chattering away like chipmunks.

"Grandmother, will you teach us how to make your delicious biscuits?" I asked.

All conversation stopped.

"Of course." Grandmother left her open suitcase on the sofa and headed toward the kitchen. "We'll make some to go with supper."

We followed Grandmother into the kitchen. I'm sure Mother wanted another chance to learn the formula. Or perhaps hoped the biscuit-making gene that had skipped her resided in her daughters.

Grandmother walked us through the steps—the first time for Kathy and me, the hundredth for Mother—even the precise way to pinch the salt and sprinkle it into the dry ingredients.

Kathy and I took turns cutting the biscuits, using a drinking glass dusted with flour. We placed each one onto the cookie sheet as though handling fine china.

Mother slipped the cookie sheet into the oven, a

prayerful look on her face.

We sat at the kitchen table and chatted, sneaking frequent peeks toward the oven. My mouth watered as the aroma of baking biscuits filled the room.

The buzzer sounded.

Mother stiffened in her chair. Her bottom lip tucked between her teeth, she tapped her nails on the table. She held her breath, awaiting the verdict.

Grandmother hopped out of her chair and strode to the oven.

Mother followed with Kathy and me behind. A flicker of hope sparkled in her eyes. Did her daughters inherit her mother's infamous baking gift? Would fluffy, white, cloud-like biscuits emerge from the oven?

The moment of truth had come.

Grandmother opened the oven door and pulled out the cookie sheet. She set it on top of the stove. Twelve perfectly round, white hockey pucks stared back at us.

Mother dropped her head. The precious biscuit-making gene remained elusive.

It's a good thing we don't have to live on bread alone. If not for the "thwack biscuits" my mother made, my family would've had to wait for God's manna from heaven. But we were far from starving—despite my mother's lack of biscuit-making skills. She nourished us daily with the recipe for the Gospel of Jesus Christ.

Sock Mops and Other Simple Pleasures

Rachel Quillin

Better is a little with righteousness
than great revenues without right.
Proverbs 16:8 kjv

One summer I thought it would be good to get my kids more involved in housework. I was pretty sure they wouldn't be quite as enthusiastic about it, so I figured I'd have to sneak it into their day. Most kids love any activity involving water so that seemed like a logical place to start. Why not let them mop the kitchen floor? So I filled up a bucket with soapy water and had them all put on a clean pair of socks. They soaked their feet and skated across the floor to fun music. I'm pretty sure it didn't get superclean, but they sure had fun in the suds—they still beg for opportunities to repeat the activity.

Of course, a job like that quickly works up an appetite and requires an ice cream treat. We go through ice cream very quickly, so it is in our best interest to buy it in large buckets. Now with a large family and a not-so-large house, I have to be very careful not to accumulate an abundance of clutter, but those buckets are good for so many things. The kids never have a shortage of uses for them. In fact, shortly after mopping the kitchen floor, they were probably all using a bucket for some sort of activity that would likely end in us having to remop the floor. One or two of them were in the creek seeking out frogs, crayfish, and other treasures that would be brought to me in all of their dripping, muddy glory.

In the meantime, another son could be seen going from spot to spot across the freshly mowed grass. He would pack the grass tightly into an ice cream bucket. Once it was tightly packed, he would dump it out, thus forming a perfect "round bale." This will keep our little boy busy for literally hours. Of course, like any good farmer, he does not leave the bales in the field. He gets his wagon and pulls it around the yard collecting his bales and delivering them to his barn under his clubhouse. This "barn," I might add, also serves as the children's garden, dinosaur dig, and anything else their big imaginations conjure up.

My girls have tomboy tendencies and truly enjoy these activities as much as their brothers, but they do have a fashionista side that, although elusive, does occasionally show up. They feel like they've hit the jackpot when someone gives them a big bag of hand-me-down clothes. They analyze each item to see if it works for their wardrobes. It would seem that obtaining clothing this way is so much better than spending time going from store to store seeking just the right combination of dress and shoes.

I suppose some would call me cheap to expect my

children to be delighted in such simple things. It's true that I do desire to curb materialistic thinking in an ultra-materialistic world, but my kids aren't without some of the "fancy" things in life. They just prefer the simpler things. In her childish wisdom, my daughter informed me, "I wish we could live like Laura Ingalls."

Doing the Best He Could

PATRICIA GRAU

*"I am the LORD your God, who teaches you what is best for you,
who directs you in the way you should go."*
ISAIAH 48:17 NIV

As a new mother, I wanted the best for my son, Noah. As soon as his father and I could get him to sit still, we began reading to him. We made sure that he had a variety of music to listen to as he played. Basically, we tried to enrich his learning opportunities whenever possible. So of course when he was old enough for preschool, we carefully reviewed the local centers. I was thrilled to find that the preschool, located just a block from our home, included swimming in their curriculum.

At the end of his first semester, I anxiously anticipated the parent night, where my husband and I would see Noah's accomplishments. The classroom activities were fresh, and we felt Noah blended in nicely. Then we moved to the pool area for the swimming demonstration. I must admit I sat up a little straighter and smiled a little brighter as I awaited Noah's swimming debut. Somehow, I believed my natural abilities would have genetically passed to him. After all, I had started swimming competitively at seven and was a teaching assistant by twelve. When I glanced at my husband, he smiled and said, "Relax, dear, this is Noah's time to shine—not yours."

After the children had assembled in lines at the side of the pool, the teacher announced that each line would, on the count of three, jump in the water and swim as fast as they could across the width of the pool and back. I noticed most of the children wore flotation assists, like Noah, who was in the third and final group. I watched the other two lines of preschoolers swim for us. Most jumped in enthusiastically; however, a few grabbed their noses before braving the waters. Although most dog-paddled with their heads held high, a few children were actually stroking with their faces in the water.

I was so excited when I heard the count of three for Noah's group. All except for one child jumped in. Noah sat down on the edge of the pool and, clinging to the lip, carefully lowered himself. He cautiously dog-paddled across the pool, keeping his face out of the water. When the others in his group arrived back to the starting point, Noah was just making the turn at the halfway mark. I plastered a smile on my disbelieving face as everyone quietly waited for Noah to complete his lap.

He beamed with joy as he grabbed the edge of the pool. He then proudly proclaimed to all, "I did the best I could!"

As my husband and I clapped with the other parents, I felt such joy. Noah's accomplishments weren't about me or meeting my expectations. Noah's accomplishments in life were about him—doing the best he could, with the talents and abilities the Lord gave him.

Mother's Day—
When Children Bless You

Marcia Hornok

Her children rise up and bless her.
Proverbs 31:28 NASB

I could smell my toddler's diaper, but first I had to clean up spilled juice under the kitchen table. While I was on my hands and knees, my darling children yelled in unison, "Happy Mother's Day!"

Yes, it was a happy day, thanks to my children's delight in giving me gifts they had kept hidden all week.

First, I received Amber's crayon rendering of "My Mother," in which I looked rather glamorous. Big blue eyes, long brown hair, earrings and necklace, and the most outstanding feature—a huge smile—all forty-six teeth drawn in. Her kindergarten teacher had written out what Amber dictated: "I know my mother loves me because she cares for me, gives me food, tucks me in at night, lets me go outside on warm days. On Christmas she gives me presents."

Thanks, Amber. Could I add: "spends thirty-five hours

making me a flower girl dress"?

My middle son, Benjy, offered a decorated soap *(so that's why I had to send a dollar to school)*, and two salt dough hearts expressing love. Grinning, he handed me the letter he had written the night before. When I had checked on him, he was sitting on the edge of his bed using the bathroom footstool for a desk. "Don't look," he said. "This is for Mother's Day." What a romantic he is for a seven-year-old.

The note read: "This was my on Ida (own idea). I love you because you play games with me and tuck me in at night and pray with me. Mothers day is here. I don't know why thay hav Mothers bay. I can't tell you how much I love you. I hope you hav a good time on Mothes bay."

I did, Benjy, thanks to my thoughtful children.

Nine-year-old Jesse culminated the gift giving. He often feels upstaged by the younger kids, but here's what this "unloved" firstborn son came up with:

M is for Mercy, mercy on my mom. *O* is for One, one like you. *T* is for True love, what we share. *H* is for Hornok, what we are. *E* is for Easygoing, what I am (*Who's he kidding!*). *R* is for Ready, you're always ready." Then he added, "Nonfowliful."

"What does *nonfowliful* mean, Jesse?"

He gave me that look—the one I give him when I'm trying hard to be patient—and he said, "It means you don't stink."

What a relief!

Dinner and celebration now complete, the children did the dishes. Last year my glass baking dish was broken. This year they only broke one salad bowl and got the measuring spoons caught in the disposal.

Although mothering can be a thankless job where days seem endless, the years are amazingly short. Every so often, like on Mother's Day, our children rise up and bless us, making it all worthwhile.

Party Politics

S. A. FULLER

Every good and perfect gift is from above,
coming down from the Father of the heavenly lights,
who does not change like shifting shadows.
JAMES 1:17 NIV

Even with both of my parents working, buying groceries and keeping current with the rent was still a struggle. We never had extra money for the one thing I wanted: a birthday party. Instead, I got a hug and a kiss, and a heartfelt reminder to make a wish. Every year I'd wish the same thing—that Mom would learn how to make a chocolate cake. Mom, admittedly, was a horrific cook and "couldn't bake a thing."

Glenda's mom was a gifted baker. Every year she threw Glenda a birthday party and baked her the most scrumptious chocolate cake I'd ever eaten.

Glenda's classmates and I were always invited to her party, but it was understood that if we came, we had to bring Glenda a gift. This coercion didn't go over well with our parents, especially Mom, who pointed out that birthdays weren't for presents but for "growing closer to our purpose." We knew she was right but refused to let anything stand between us and candlelit chocolate bliss.

After devouring the cake and drinking our weight in cherry Kool-Aid, we'd gather to watch Glenda open her presents. Before she'd unwrap any gifts, she'd riffle through them, shake a few, and then quiz the group. "Whose is this? What about this?"

She'd ask specifically about the biggest one and the smallest.

Glenda savored this part of the party, though she hadn't always.

During the pre-chocolate-cake era, most kids played Glenda's party for laughs. They'd come sweaty and smelly, straight from the playground, with nothing more thoughtful than a broken yo-yo, a worn bingo card, or a tattered jump rope. Back then, the featured cake was a pasty-icing, store-bought version. Once it was replaced with Glenda's mom's baked chocolate goodness, everything changed. Glenda's party became a dress-up affair, and everyone was held to a higher standard of gifting.

After Glenda found out who'd brought practically every gift, she'd rip through wrapping paper faster than you could say "surprise." She squealed with delight if she opened a keeper—a novelty of high value and general appeal. When she tore into anything she didn't like, she'd stuff it back into its wrapper and toss it aside as if it never existed.

After all the gifts had been opened, she'd survey the

room and ask, "Who didn't bring anything?" No one needed to confess. She knew who they were and pointed them out.

Both the embarrassed and those of us who'd managed to gift to her expectations endured her uncomfortable interrogation because the chocolate cake was that good. If my wish came true and Mom could bake one as delicious, then I'd be the one drowning in presents on my birthday. No matter how many gifts I got, I'd never be as judgmental or ungrateful as Glenda. I would insist that no one even bring me a gift unless they wanted to.

Eventually I stopped wasting my wishes on chocolate cakes. Mom's cooking actually improved. She even tried to bake a chocolate cake. It was a gallant effort, but not an edible one. Still, I love her for trying and for teaching me that a birthday is a celebration with gifts or without them.

Life Is Not a Beach

S. A. FULLER

*But if you harbor bitter envy and selfish ambition in your hearts,
do not boast about it or deny the truth. Such "wisdom"
does not come down from heaven but is earthly, unspiritual,
demonic. For where you have envy and selfish ambition,
there you find disorder and every evil practice.*

JAMES 3:14–16 NIV

The highlight of my summer was when my favorite cousin, Margaret, came to town. Margaret's mom was my mom's older sister. Aunt Betty moved to Miami after marrying and came home to visit every summer. Margaret was smart and carefree and made all her own clothes. She was fifteen years old this trip, a year older than me.

I was set for a blast, but Margaret didn't want to do much more than sit in the rocking chairs on our grandmother's screen porch and talk. I'd been sweating through one of the city's hottest summers. She was still getting used to our suffocating heat and humidity. I was devastated that Margaret wasn't enjoying herself, but there was nothing I could do about the weather.

Later Margaret confessed that the source of her blues wasn't the heat. She missed her friends. With no scheduled summer concerts or block parties, her vacation in our small hometown felt more like punishment. Then she told me about the fun we both could be having at any one of her favorite beaches, parks, or shopping malls. I was so thrilled to be included in her wishful brooding that I joined her in complaining about all that we were missing.

Margaret started to cheer up. We spent the rest of the summer on the porch comparing hometowns and wishing we were at the beach. By the time summer ended, we'd determined that I deserved to live in the better city and had to come stay with her family.

We figured school would be Mom's only argument against the arrangement, but based on our comparisons, Margaret's school was bigger, the lunches were tastier, and the students were wittier. I was sure to learn more in a school like that. Margaret volunteered to make my school clothes and insisted I ride back with them when they left the following weekend.

Three days later, I still didn't feel rehearsed enough to convince Mom to let me go. She'd never agreed to any of my propositions before. With the help of Margaret's brainpower, I felt I had an answer to every possible objection. This time, I was almost certain she had to say *yes*. She didn't. She rattled off something about families needing to stay together, financial burdens, and if I got sick. . .

I'd tuned out.

The images in my head of frolicking on the beach and

spending more time with Margaret faded to black. She and her family went home without me. I stopped speaking to Mom. Eventually I went back to playing with my old friends, riding bikes, playing hide-and-seek, enjoying hopscotch, winning dodgeball. We didn't notice the heat. We just had fun.

I couldn't stay mad at Mom for long, especially when she was extra nice to me. I got ice cream every day for a whole week. I wasn't so ready to pack my bags after that. I was glad to be home.

Mom's Survival Guide:
Love

Girls-in-Berry

ANITA HIGMAN

Jesus said, "Let the little children come to me,
and do not hinder them, for the kingdom
of heaven belongs to such as these."
MATTHEW 19:14 NIV

When I was a kid, there was this TV show called *Art Linkletter's House Party*, and one segment featured impromptu interviews with children. Those kids said the most delightful and unexpected things imaginable. In fact, their answers to the host's questions sent audiences into fits of laughter.

That is the magic of all kids. And both my children had that same enchantment. So much so that when they were growing up, I started writing down what they said—those precious one-of-a-kind gems that you want to repeat someday to *their* children. When my son, Scott, was very young, he had trouble pronouncing the word *spaghetti*. So when he was ready to eat a mound of pasta, he always asked for the "pee-sketty." Okay, isn't that just too cute?

And then my daughter, Hillary, when she was a

wee one, thought it was odd that she'd only heard about boysenberries. So with a quizzical expression, she asked me, "Why aren't there any girls-in-berries?" Good question.

Along with the adorable sayings and queries, children are also full of creativity and innocence and startling honesty. And then there's that other amazing quality kids have—guilelessness.

Jesus loved children, and He, too, loved a child's innocent heart. So much so that He told His disciples that they were not to hinder the children from coming to Him. I can just imagine that the little ones ran up to Him, snuggled on His lap, and waited for a hug or a story or both. But Jesus also gave His disciples another nugget of truth in His request. He said that the kingdom of heaven belonged to those who had that same kind of childlike heart. Countless times I've asked God to give me a spirit of guilelessness. It is the quality Jesus so appreciated in His disciple Nathanael. And it is what I long for.

So many times I can become entangled in a dark world of cynical beliefs, selfish pursuits, and harsh retorts. Sinful ways can stick to my soul as tenaciously as chewing gum to the sole of my shoe.

So, what's a mom to do then? May my daily prayer be, "Lord, wash me clean of all that keeps me from Your light. All that keeps me from being innocent before You. All that keeps me from climbing onto Your lap like a child and sharing my heart and love with You. Amen."

That's Easy for You to Say

JANET ROCKEY

If I speak with the tongues of men and of angels,
but do not have love, I have become
a noisy gong or a clanging cymbal.
1 CORINTHIANS 13:1 NASB

I left my Child Psychology class with a happy heart. At last, the speech anomaly that plagued the women in my family had a name—dyspraxia. My excitement bubbled as I called my sister, Kathy, on the way to my car in the University of Tampa parking lot.

"Guess what I learned tonight?" I asked when Kathy answered her phone. Giving her no opportunity to respond, I blurted out, "Psychologists have a name for when we get our merds wixed. It's Praxdysia!" *Groan.* I did it again. "No. I mean it's called. . .dyspraxia."

I grew up believing Mother, Kathy, and I were the only people who suffered with this challenge. I recall as a child standing in the laundry detergent section of the store with Mom. She stopped a clerk walking by and asked, "Where is the sobbric fastener?"

"What?" The young man looked at her like she had lobsters crawling out of her ears.

"You know, Downy."

The clerk took a step back. "Oh, Downy," he said. "Fabric softener. It–it's on the next aisle." He darted away.

Another incident occurred at a service station where, back in the 1960s, a teenage boy pumped your gas, checked your oil, and washed your windshield. The power steering column in Mother's 1960 Oldsmobile developed a slow leak. She drove into the nearby service station and pulled to a stop next to the pump. The gas jockey trotted out to meet her.

"Would you check the flower peering stuid, please?"

He gave her the same look as the clerk in the store. "Check what, ma'am?"

"The stuff. . .for. . ." she sputtered and pointed to the steering wheel.

"Oh, right," he said with a nod. "Power steering fluid."

We weren't sure if the disorder was inherited or contagious. My sister, Kathy, always heralded the spring season with, "Happy Equal Vernox!" To this day, she still can't say *vernal equinox*. I've always enjoyed Ruffles chitayta pips with my sandwiches. "Po-ta-to chips." I had to sound out each syllable when ordering in a deli. Mother often invited a friend over for a morning coff of cuppee.

One day my husband offered to take me shopping. "Want to go to Starnmite?" He took on the same gaze as the clerk and the gas jockey of the old days. "What did just say?" Bubbles appeared in front of his eyes. He had to sit down.

I chuckled. "You mean *Steinmart*?"

The Child Psychology professor explained it in layman's terms. The words form correctly in the brain but get twisted in the transference from mind to mouth.

Mother accepted her affliction with a shrug and a giggle. The oddest facet to this glitch in her conversational skills is it never interfered with her ability to say tongue twisters. Peter Piper always picked his peck of pickled peppers perfectly, and the little girl continued to sell seashells by the seashore.

Though her speech may have sounded like a noisy gong or clanging cymbal to those unfamiliar with dyspraxia, Mother never mixed up her words when she told me about the love of Jesus. And if she fumbled her verbal prayers, the Lord understood. He knew her heart.

This story illustrates a mild case of dyspraxia, and in no way is intended to make light of those who struggle with the more serious effects of this disorder.

A Loaf and Some Fish

JEAN FISCHER

A wife of noble character who can find?
She is worth far more than rubies.
PROVERBS 31:10 NIV

The year was 1941, and my mom was a new bride. She and Dad scraped together enough money for a down payment on a house, and in July they moved into an old bungalow on the west shore of Lake Michigan.

Mom settled into her role as a wife. She was just nineteen, and she didn't have much experience with cooking and housekeeping. Mom learned the hard way how much starch to put in Dad's shirts and how long to roast a chicken. Cooking was not her strong point, and often their dog, Shivers, enjoyed dinner more than Dad did.

Early one morning, Dad went fishing and returned with a string of perch. "Honey," he announced, "let's have a fish fry tonight!"

The color drained from Mom's face. Dad didn't notice. He plopped the fish into the kitchen sink and went to get ready for work. Mom had no idea what to do with the slippery dead bodies. She wouldn't admit that to Dad though. When he left for work, she kissed him and promised him a wonderful supper.

Mom washed the fish in cold water and put them in the icebox. Later she'd figure out what to do with them. In the meantime, she'd bake bread. That was something she was good at. She mixed the dough and left it to rise. Then she took a bath.

While she was in the tub, Shivers barked at the bathroom door. Mom recognized that he was desperate to do his business. So she got out of the tub, threw on a bathrobe, and hurried with Shivers to the door. The dog rushed on ahead, nearly knocking her over. The door slammed shut, locking them out.

Naked under her bathrobe, Mom was reluctant to go for help. It took an hour before she found a way to break into the house. Not a great start to her day.

By late afternoon, things were better. The house smelled of freshly baked bread, and she'd set the table to look special. Everything was ready, except for the fish. Mom vaguely remembered her mother frying fish in a pan on the stove with some butter, salt, and pepper. How hard could it be? She got out the frying pan, melted some butter, and fried the perch—whole!

When Dad arrived home, there was the platter of perch on the table, fish eyes eerily staring up at him.

"Honey," he said softly. "Don't you know that you have to clean and filet them first?"

Mom cried. Dad hugged her. "It's all right, dear," he said. "You'll learn."

The Bible says, "Let all that you do be done with love" (1 Corinthians 16:14 NKJV). Sometimes what we do in love is less than perfect, but in doing, we learn. Like most young couples, Mom and Dad learned. And for sixty-eight years, they enjoyed Mom's fish fries.

Racing for Mom

MARCIA HORNOK

In this is love, not that we loved God,
but that He loved us.
1 JOHN 4:10 NKJV

I'm going to win the Race for the Cure this year—for you, Mom," Nathan told me. I knew he could do it. He had recently set a new record for the Park City (Utah) Marathon and had won three half-marathons, one of them against 4,600 runners. The Susan G. Komen 5K race, for breast cancer research, would not be difficult for him to win.

In that race, only the first-place runner receives recognition and gets interviewed on the radio. It warmed my heart that Nathan wanted to honor me one month after my breast-cancer treatments had ended.

On the morning of the race, I waited for Nathan about a quarter mile from the finish line. Perhaps my cheering would give him the extra kick a winner needs at the end.

My excitement swelled when the first runner turned a corner and came down the street where I waited. But it was not Nathan. About thirty yards behind that fleet fellow was my son. As Nathan came within earshot, I yelled some encouragement: "I love you, Nathan!" He broke into a grin as he sped by.

Later he told me what went through his mind at that point: *Do I have enough reserve to pass that guy? Is he as tired as I am? I want to do this for Mom. Can I possibly run harder?* Then he recalled my words and concluded, *Mom will love me whether I win this race or not.* He came in second and got no recognition. Except from me.

He honored me by how hard he tried and by his desire to please me. Whether he earns any trophies or not, he has a *first place* in my heart. His thinking was accurate—I'm his mother—I will love him no matter what.

Sometimes I attempt to prove my love for God by achieving certain self-imposed goals: singing a solo in the worship service, having the best-behaved children, spending the most hours volunteering at school. I have a tendency to compare myself with my friends and try to come in *first* through how my house looks, in my parenting skills, or by taking the best casserole to the church dinner. As if God will love me more if I do extra credit or surpass other moms.

I need to remember that God loves me because of who He is, not what I do for Him. His love is relationship based, not dependent on how I perform. It never fails and never fluctuates. Yes, He wants my best efforts and rewards my faithfulness and endurance, but He looks at motivation more than achievement.

Therefore I honor Him best by running my life race in communion with Him as I do my daily tasks. My goal is to enjoy God's unconditional love and not try to earn it.

Testing the Waters

Donna K. Maltese

Anyone who meets a testing challenge head-on
and manages to stick it out is mighty fortunate.
For such persons loyally in love with God,
the reward is life and more life.
James 1:12 MSG

Many children go through a rebellious stage in their teen years. I myself gave my mother many a gray hair with my shenanigans. Then, when I began having children of my own, it seemed to be payback time.

When my son, Zach, entered kindergarten and my daughter, Jen, began her freshman year of high school, I got part-time work as the church secretary. During my third year there, Jen began testing the waters of parental authority. It began with little things—staying out later than allowed, neglecting schoolwork, etc. This was also a period during which Jen spent lots of time in her room with the door shut, in addition to doing plenty of eye rolling, heavy sighing, and arguing.

One spring weekday, my boss, Pastor Geib, having just

come back from lunch at the local diner, entered my office.

Seated at my desk, I looked up at him. "How was your lunch?"

"Lunch? Um, fine, fine."

We then began discussing the projects I was working on, along with some other things. Finally, during a lull in our conversation, he paused and shuffled his feet a bit.

Hmm.

"Yes, Pastor? What's up?"

"Well, I was just wondering. . . . Is today an in-service day at the high school?"

"No."

"Is it a school holiday or something like that?"

"No. . . Why?"

"Well, I went to the Sellersville diner today. . . . "

"Yes? And?"

"I saw your daughter, Jen, there."

My heart sank to my knees. "Really."

"Yep. I wasn't sure whether or not I should tell you."

"Did she see you?"

"Oh yeah. I even said hello."

"Hmm. And how did she react?"

"Well, she wasn't very happy."

Of all the people to run into, Jen had collided with Pastor Geib. Needless to say, we grounded her for cutting school. And Jen's rebellion continued into her late teens. But we all survived. And even better than that, she is now one of the sweetest, most loving, responsible young adults I know.

Yes, our children will test our limits and try our

patience. And as they go through this period of adjustment, we will find ourselves channeling our own parents, saying things like, "Just because everybody else is doing it doesn't mean it's right." "I've had it up to here with you." "As long as you're living under our roof, you'll follow our rules." "The subject is closed." "If you're going to pout, go up to your room and do it." "Someday you'll have children of your own and they'll be just like you." "You're not going anywhere until you clean up your room."

And the list goes on and on.

The key to parenting is to pepper our admonishments with love and affection, no matter how unlovable our children seem at the time. And before we know it, we'll have weathered the storm to find that our children have grown into lovely adults who will one day have children of their own.

Adoptions and Doll Nurseries

VALORIE QUESENBERRY

*So you have not received a spirit that makes you fearful slaves.
Instead, you received God's Spirit when he adopted you
as his own children. Now we call him, "Abba, Father."*
ROMANS 8:15 NLT

The year she was nine, my second daughter saved up her birthday and Christmas money to buy a doll at a special doll nursery. It was a full-service event. She looked over the babies in their little nursery baskets through a big window. Then she was escorted in to choose the one she wanted. Next, the "nurse" took her to the desk where she received special instructions and filled out paperwork including an official adoption certificate.

She was a radiant mommy. The "grandmother" (me) took pictures of the happy occasion—I guess even pretend grandmas have to get out the camera. She left that place happy as she could be with her baby held closely in her arms.

But the good times weren't over. Since this doll wore actual baby clothing in size three months, the new mommy had a perpetual desire to go shopping. And the baby was now included in family outings and even trips to the grocery store. Though my youngest was then three years old, I now had another "baby" in a carrier sitting in my shopping cart. More than once, the doll was mistaken for a real infant, much to the astonishment of other shoppers who were somewhat appalled that I was not being more attentive to the newborn lying haphazardly in the carrier.

You could say that this doll adoption changed not only my daughter's life but mine as well. Even my husband got in on the fun as our daughter insisted he take a turn holding his new "grandchild."

But a doll adoption can't even begin to compare with the real thing. I have a good friend who recently became an adoptive mother. She and her husband yearned and prayed and completed lengthy amounts of paperwork. Then they made multiple trips to court. Then they prayed some more and asked others to pray with them about the obstacles that stood in the way of their future. Finally, the day came when the judge pounded the gavel and announced that they had a new daughter. For my friend and her family, that was a day beyond compare. It's difficult to hear her describe the event without feeling a bit weepy.

So, just imagine what joy the Father takes in our adoption into His family! He went to the trouble to rescue us and redeem us. He gave His Son to make the necessary payment. He made all the arrangements.

And He waits for our consent.

When that day comes, He rejoices. He writes a new

entry in the family registry. And He lavishes the new son or daughter with His tender love and constant nearness.

Adoptions are an act of love. Whether the receiver of that love is a doll, a tiny baby, or a human soul, the adoption is initiated by the one making the choice. I'm thankful our God believes in adoption. And I'm glad He let me see a little of His Fatherly joy reflected on my daughter's face that day in the doll nursery.

Contributing Authors

RENAE BRUMBAUGH lives in Texas with her two noisy children and two dogs. She's authored four books in Barbour's Camp Club Girls series, *Morning Coffee with James* (Chalice Press), and has contributed to several anthologies. Her humor column and articles have appeared in publications across the country.

JEAN FISCHER has been writing for nearly three decades and has worked as an editor with Golden Books. She has cowritten with Thomas Kinkade and John MacArthur, and is one of the authors for Barbour's Camp Club Girls series. Recent books include the *Kids' Bible Dictionary* and *199 Bible People, Places, and Things*.

S. A. FULLER is a freelance writer living in Atlanta, Georgia, who's matured enough to appreciate a life's worth of mom wisdom that initially provoked shameless eye rolling. Now that it has all come true, so, too, has the deep regret for being a hardheaded know-it-all and the whole-hearted belief that there's a bit of genius in all mothers.

PATRICIA GRAU is a retired engineer. After years of technical writing, she has moved into fiction. While active in her church and community, Pat's main focus is her family. She and her husband are Michigan residents who spend their winters in Florida. They have four children and nine grandchildren.

JANICE HANNA hails from south Texas. She is a Christian author and mother of four grown daughters. Janice has written over forty books, most under the name Janice A. Thompson.

Bestselling and award-winning author ANITA HIGMAN has over thirty books published (several coauthored) for adults and children. She's been a Barnes & Noble "Author of the Month" for Houston and has a BA degree, combining speech communication, psychology, and art. Anita loves good movies, exotic teas, and brunch with her friends.

MARCIA HORNOK, managing editor of *CHERA* magazine for widows/ers, raised six children in Salt Lake City, where her husband pastors Midvalley Bible Church. She has numerous publishing credits in periodicals, devotional books, and online.

ARDYTHE KOLB is a freelance writer and is on the board of Heart of America Christian Writers' Network. She and her husband owned a successful Christian bookstore while they raised five children. She loves spending time with family and friends, and enjoys travel, reading, target practice, and painting.

TINA KRAUSE is the author of *Laughter Therapy*, Barbour's *Grand Moments for Grandmothers*, *The Bible Promise Book for Women*, *Life is Sweet*, and *God's Answers for Your Life— Parents' Edition*. She is a contributor to over twenty-three book compilations and has nine hundred published writing credits. A freelance writer and award-winning newspaper columnist, Tina lives with her husband, Jim, in Valparaiso, Indiana where they enjoy spoiling their five grandchildren.

DONNA K. MALTESE is a freelance writer, editor, and writing coach. Mother of two grown children, she resides in Bucks County, Pennsylvania, with her husband. Donna is active in her local church and is the publicist for a local Mennonite project that works to feed the hungry here and abroad.

VALORIE QUESENBERRY is a pastor's wife, mother, musician, editor of a Christian ladies' magazine, and a writer. She periodically contributes devotionals to a Christian literature provider. Her first book released with Wesleyan Publishing House in April 2010.

RACHEL QUILLIN is the author of several gift books and coauthor of the devotional prayer book *Prayers & Promises for Mothers*. She makes her home on a dairy farm in Stonecreek, Ohio, with her husband and children.

Janet Rockey is a member of FWA, ACFW, and Word Weavers. She has studied under authors Gayle Roper, Jeanette Windle, and Mark Mynheir at Florida Christian Writers Conferences. Janet lives with her husband, Tom, and their two cats in Tampa, Florida. Visit her blog at rockeywrites.blogspot.com.

OLD TESTAMENT